THE OTHER NORMAL

Understanding Asperger's

JEANETTE D. HARMON

PublishAmerica
Baltimore

KH

First printing

PublishAmerica has allowed this work to remain exactly as the author intended, verbatim, without editorial input.

Hardcover 978-1-4560-6047-3
Softcover 978-1-4560-6048-0
PUBLISHED BY PUBLISHAMERICA, LLLP
www.publishamerica.com
Baltimore

Printed in the United States of America

10/17/11

ACKNOWLEDGEMENTS

I have been so extremely blessed in my life and being able to write this book is surely one of those blessings. I would have never been able to complete it without the help of so many good friends who spent hours reading, editing, and encouraging. I want to personally thank each one of them: JoAnne Martinez, Teresa Dunford, Kellie Cowley, Debbie Bowen, Kathy Bell, Billy Stark, Donna Linson, and Michelle Emery. All of you have been some of my greatest supporters and I value your input and your friendships.

A special thank you to Brandy Slagle for taking the time to share her many thoughts, feelings, ideas and opinions. She gave me many insights about her son that added to the book.

I want to thank my family for putting up with my endless questions and for all of their helpful suggestions for the book. I want to acknowledge all of my daughter Tonisha's help on the computer getting things just right. I could not have done this without her! She also helped me with the research and contributed more than she realizes. I want to thank my oldest son R.J. for his continuous support and encouragement. He always knew I could do this. I thank my sweet husband Bob for all his patience and unlimited time he gave up with me while I worked on this endeavor. He was my greatest fan and encouraged me all along to complete this book.

Most of all, I want to thank Jesse. Without him there would not be The Other Normal. He adds so much enjoyment to our family. We are so blessed to have a son who has Asperger's and get to see firsthand some of the different ways he views the world. He is the most nonjudgmental, kind and generous person I know.

CONTENTS

PREFACE

November 9, 2004 (Jeanette's journal entry)

*I am a little concerned about just realizing after all these years that Jesse has Asperger's (I had actually called it autism because that's what I thought it was in the beginning). I am reading everything I can get my hands on, and **then** I will take him to a doctor. He just really seems so much more advanced than I would think, but a lot of the signs are definitely there. His constant hand swinging; he won't carry a conversation; and he talks mostly in fragments instead of whole sentences. But he is such a good, sweet, smart kid. We could not ask for a better child! Jesse's first 7th grade report card (this year) was straight A's! He has always been such a giving and caring boy and does just about everything he is told.*

Those were my first thoughts, six years ago, when our story began. Today Jesse is a very well-rounded, smart, talented, friendly, "normal" nineteen year old boy! By the way, I despise the word normal because how does anyone define what normal is? Regardless, Jesse has come a very long way since early childhood and is incredibly victorious! He talks a lot more as he has gotten older and puts much more effort into socializing. I have learned so much since that first realization in November of 2004. I hope that through this book I can help others who are either just finding out about someone they love or who have even been struggling with Autism Spectrum Disorder (ASD) for years to understand it better and to realize all the potential this challenge has to offer. Those who have ASD have some special gifts that the rest of us should respect and admire. I am not saying it is easy to live with ASD by any means, but many of our dreams for our children with ASD, as well as their own, can and do come true! When they do it is even more rewarding because of the distinctive struggles they conquered to get there.

Most people, including virtually every professional, include Asperger's on the ASD scale as high functioning autism. What I have learned through research for this book has convinced me that Asperger's is more removed from autism than most realize. They have so many similar characteristics that it is almost impossible to talk about one without including the other, but the *intensity* of the traits between the two seem *very* different. Autism is usually much more apparent than Asperger's. To keep it less complicated I will mostly use the terms ASD or AS (Asperger's) throughout this book. My son has AS and that is what this book generally focuses on, so we can't assume children with autism will be entirely the same. Autism and Asperger's are both neurological as well as physical disorders, and there are no clear answers to what causes them or if they can be fully cured. There have been some instances where parents insist their children have been cured.

Although I use the male gender throughout the book the condition is not exclusive to boys. It is much more common in boys, but typically when a girl has ASD her condition is much more severe than most boys who have it. Research has not been able to prove why that is at this point.

I have read many very interesting, touching, and frightening stories about different families experiences with ASD's, but never one that even comes close to our story. Every child's condition is as different as every child is. There are similarities in children with AS but there are also many differences in each child. However, I haven't heard of anyone not realizing there was something different about their own child clear until their teens, like we did! That is part of the reason I decided to write this book. I can't be the only one in my shoes! (A metaphor that someone with AS wouldn't get). I am hoping that through Jesse others will be able to feel connected to us and share a few laughs as well as hopes. Those families with children on the extreme end of the spectrum would have very different experiences to share than ours; and those with children who are "recovered" would also have a much different story. Jesse's is one of hope for parents, like me, who did not know early enough to get intervention and treatments but still have many successes to share.

I did not write this book as an autobiography of Jesse's life because not knowing he was "different" clear until his early teens would leave out a lot. I try to show through many family antidotes throughout that we have had a very amazing and interesting journey with Jesse's AS since learning of it, and an abundance of success. Along with sharing some of my families experiences with AS, I have included a lot of information about the topic in general. I will explain some of the symptoms and conditions that these kids, and adults, live with. My hope is to help inform more people of what AS really is and what a gift those who have it are.

This book is for anyone who has a child of their own with ASD, anyone who knows someone with it, or anyone who lives on this planet! ASD's have reached such colossal numbers that every single one of us at some point will associate with someone who has the disorder, and every one of us should know and understand more about it so that we can help them have the best life possible. The life they deserve.

When I first realized that Jesse has AS, it really didn't change anything. I wasn't too concerned because he had always had friends, did very well in school, was obedient at home and in public, and had always been very independent. He seems to get along just fine in the world and had a pretty normal childhood. I figured, so what if he has a few quirks, he is a really great kid! It wasn't until later, when I started researching more about the condition that I realized what it really meant. What troubles me now is how *he* feels and what *he* has to go through basically every moment of every day! He must live a very confusing and stressful life that people who know little or nothing about AS would just not even realize. Even those of us who do understand the symptoms of AS cannot *really* know what it must be like for our kids. These people are courageous, strong individuals! My son is a hero. I am proud of Jesse and respect him so much for dealing with everything he does endlessly just to correspond with this human race.

The spectrum is so broad and still so unknown that at this point ASD is a widely complicated and often misunderstood disorder. Until essentially the last decade it had been very easily misdiagnosed. It can still take up to five or more wrong diagnoses to finally see an ASD as the problem. And with the spectrum of ASD's being so large, it can be really difficult to narrow it down to which one the child may have. ASD's are finally beginning to gain more public recognition in the 21st century because many believe it has become an epidemic. In 2007 the rate of a new child being diagnosed with autism was 1 in every 150 children. If that was not disturbing enough, only three years later the statistics are showing closer to 1 in 100. I can easily believe this knowing that I have a neighbor, and friend, only two houses away that has a son with AS, as well as another friend right across the street whose grandson has it.

That is three of us living right within feet of each other. How many more children or adults are there right here in my little neighborhood with ASD I wonder?

A lot of things are different when your child is diagnosed at thirteen compared to three. Many experts say that early intervention is vital if you expect any success or even possibly a full cure of ASD; but knowing what I know now, I don't believe that. I believe there is always hope. What choice would I have anyway? My son is well past the established "window of opportunity". I have recognized huge progress in Jesse's life since finding out only six years ago, at the age of thirteen. We have not had any intervention at all other than what we have tried to do for Jesse as his family and what he has done for himself. We did try to find some help with speech and social development at fourteen and were basically told he did not need it. "He was not bad enough" to qualify for help. Jesse was doing very well in a mainstream junior high school academically and also had many friends. But that is not to say therapy would not have helped him. He still has a hard time with communication, though he is greatly improving the older he gets, which gives me a lot of hope for his future. Jesse will answer short questions and respond much better than he did at a younger age, but he still does not often carry a conversation more than a few sentences. He doesn't offer free information either. Typical children will give you every detail of an experience where Jesse will not even mention it if not asked specifically.

I wrote this book with the intention of bringing faith, happiness and gratitude to families dealing with ASD, along with more education to the general public. There are so many wonderful gifts these children can share with us and things they can teach us. My intentions are never to downplay or appear unfeeling to the thousands of families who deal with so many excruciating issues every day of their lives because of this disorder. This, being a spectrum disorder, means a very wide range of symptoms clear from the child being nonverbal and in a world we cannot seem to break into, to the other end where the child is in mainstream school without any help and hardly anyone knowing they even have a disability. Every parent dealing with ASD wishes for one main thing: to reach their child and be able to communicate with them. No matter what level of the spectrum our children are on, every one of us deal with this in one way or another. I cannot even envision how painful it would be to never hear the words "mommy or daddy" from your child. Happily, many parents in this situation have learned other ways to bond with their child.

While I do not face some of the greater issues common to ASD, I do face enough to know that it is hard on some level for everyone involved. Every one of us worries about what the future holds for our child. We worry if they will get married, have children, have good jobs, be independent, be happy, and most of all be accepted. Many parents must also worry about who will take care of their child after they are gone. There are many concerns, which fortunately, are beginning to be addressed more every day. We need the public to be educated in understanding and accepting our children and in helping them to fit into their confusing world. This may give them more opportunities at having an independent successful life with the help of kind and understanding people. A lot of these individuals are very capable, and the higher functioning ones are an asset to the working community as they are generally very responsible, intelligent, hardworking and honest people.

My hope is that all of society will recognize what an amazing gift our children with ASD are and that with our love and support they can accomplish unimaginable things! If it were just for me, I would not change a single thing about Jesse because I think he is pretty perfect just the way he is. But for him, I would love for him not to have to deal with the difficulties of AS. I know it would make his life unbelievably easier if he did not have to struggle day in and day out trying to follow what people are saying, and always feeling that he is different. I believe his challenges bless him and make him a better person, as well as those who are fortunate enough to know him. Jesse is a very loving and nonjudgmental person who wants to do everything he can to enhance his own life as well as that of others.

We can all keep hoping and praying for more research to uncover all the unknowns of ASD and someday find a resolution for every one of these children, as well as adults. But as we wait for that day to come, we must find a good support system and relish every bit of hope we do receive. Enjoy the uniqueness of your child and the person that they are. Their ASD is just another element of them.

CHAPTER ONE

Finding Out

Along with all of Jesse's unusual attributes came so many amazing ones that I just always knew we had a very special and unique son. I never once thought of him having a disorder of any kind. It never even crossed my mind that his horrible tantrums at age two were not just "the terrible two's"; or that all the time he spent alone in his room instead of playing with friends during his elementary years was not because he was just extremely good at entertaining himself. The fact that he was totally potty trained before he was even two years old then started having many daily accidents a year or so later was not just laziness (we did see a doctor). I do have to admit that when I would find him as a toddler curled up in a ball lying on a shelf in our dark, cold, food storage room I was a little concerned. And he did that quite often. But even then I thought he was just trying to hide because he was upset and wanted to be left alone. Which was actually probably true.

How could a mother not know something is different about her own child? I always thought he did some funny, quirky things but was still just like everyone else. Jesse is not even our first or only child, so I did have others to compare him to. He has a brother, R.J., who is two years older and a sister, Tonisha, two years younger. I just thought he was always a little more of a loner and chose not to be as sociable as his siblings since he spent so much time alone. Jesse did have friends after all; he just chose to be alone. I figured he was a very deep individual, a thinker. Not every child needed to be entertained by friends every second of the day.

I was at my dad's house one afternoon standing in the driveway talking with him when he suddenly brought up Jesse. Nobody else had ever said anything, so I was totally shocked, and honestly quite irritated, when my own dad suggested something was wrong with my child! He said, as gentle as he could manage, "Do you think Jesse could be autistic?" I gave him a quick and unequivocal "No!" How could he think something so ridiculous? I immediately pictured a child sitting on a floor up against the wall rocking and banging their head.

"Jesse talks all the time and is really smart!" I started to defend him with all the fierceness of a mother lioness. "He is really obedient and does everything we ask. He has friends and does really well in school. Everybody loves him!"

My dad's only reply was, "They can be really smart and do very well in school and life…I just notice some things that make me wonder."

It would only be a couple of weeks before I came to appreciate my dad's courage to actually say to me what many others had been thinking. I can't blame them for not bringing it up…who wants to tell someone their child is different?

Ironically, I was at a doctor's office a couple of weeks later reading an article in the *Readers Digest* where a father was trying to figure out what was wrong with his son and soon found out it was ASD (autism spectrum disorder). As I read, all I could think was, "Wow! This story could be titled *'Jesse's Life'*!" It explained the hand flapping (even though he didn't do that very often), the monotone speech, the obsession with Lego's and dinosaurs, the confusion about how to use the telephone, his huge problem with gooey-textured foods, and his need to spend so much time alone in his room. This was the beginning of a whole new world for me, and in many ways him. I wanted to know everything I could about ASD and understand what Jesse must be going through as much as possible. I had no idea what it all really meant.

Unexpectedly, when I told my husband Bob, he believed me. We had never even once in Jesse's thirteen years said a single word to one another about anything being out of the ordinary with our son. I don't think Bob realized how serious this was or what it really meant at first, but then neither did I. But he believed me, and that is what mattered. My husband has always been very supportive and he appreciates and respects all of my research, ideas, feelings, and suggestions of ways to help Jesse. Bob has the same concerns and fears as I do, but he is a lot easier going about them than I am. He is very optimistic about how well Jesse does and believes he will do just fine in life, which gives me more reassurance also.

When a parent first finds out that their child has ASD they usually have an overwhelming feeling of urgency. They rush to read everything they can get hold of on the subject, look up everything possible on the internet, and sometimes join discussion groups. It can become overwhelming to try to learn everything all at once. There is so much to absorb and much of it is depressing and spirit-sapping. There are professionals to consult, schools to find, therapy, medication, and special diets to consider. And how to pay for it all! Don't allow yourself to get overwhelmed. You have time. You have *a lot* of time! You have next month and next year and every year after that. Every day, every week, and every year brings new information for researchers and for you. Your child is most likely not going anywhere. He is the same person he was the day before you found out and he will be the same person tomorrow. Try to keep things in perspective and know that we all adjust to what life throws at us.

I found a very thoughtful essay written by children's author Emily Perl Kingsley who is the mother of a child with Down syndrome. She illustrates beautifully what it is like to be the mother of a child who brings a different expectation:

"Welcome to Holland"

When you are going to have a baby it's like planning a fabulous vacation trip to Italy. You buy a bunch of guide books and make your wonderful plans. The Coliseum, The Michelangelo David, The gondolas in Venice. You may learn some handy phrases in Italian. It's all very exciting.

After months of eager anticipation, the day finally arrives. You pack your bags and off you go. Several hours later the plane lands and the stewardess comes in and says "Welcome to Holland."

"Holland?!?" you say. "What do you mean Holland???"

"I signed up for Italy! I'm supposed to be in Italy! All my life I've dreamed of going to Italy."

But there's been a change in the flight plan. They have landed in Holland and there you must stay. The important thing is that they haven't taken you to a horrible, disgusting, filthy place full of pestilence, famine or disease. It's just a different place.

So you must go out and buy new guide books. And you must learn a whole new language. And you will meet a whole new group of people you would have never met.

It's just a different place. It's slower-paced than Italy, less flashy than Italy. But after you've been there for a while and catch your breath, you look around...and you will begin to notice that Holland has windmills…and Holland has tulips. Holland even has Rembrandts.

But everyone you know is busy coming and going from Italy…and they're all bragging about what a wonderful time they had there. And for the rest of your life, you will say "Yes, that's where I was supposed to go. That's what I had planned."

And the pain of that will never, ever, ever go away… because the loss of that dream is a very significant loss.

But…if you spend your life mourning the fact that you didn't get to Italy, you may never be free to enjoy the very special, the very lovely things, about Holland.

It was not until years later that I realized that what Jesse has is actually Asperger's not autism. I had never even heard of Asperger's until Jesse was fifteen. It took even longer to learn that they are quite different from each other, which explained a lot of my misconceptions. Initially, I was very confused when learning that he had what we thought was autism because I was always under the impression that children with autism were most often detached and basically in a world of their own. I had always heard that they did not particularly want to be held or cuddled. Jesse was an extreme opposite to that. As a toddler he was so glued to me that, though I hate to admit it, it got very tiresome at times. Most mothers enjoy holding and cuddling with their child, but I could not even walk without him clinging to my leg. I later learned that young children with AS are quite often attached to one of their parents, most often their mother. They have intense emotional reactions to changes in routines or expectations and their mother is the constant in their lives that helps them survive it all. She is their security blanket. Ironically, though, now in his teens Jesse will not let me even sit too close to him or give him a hug. Now I miss those days when he could not get enough of me. We always seem to want the opposite of what we have…

Just knowing Jesse has AS answered so many questions for me and also made life at home a more pleasant place for all of us, especially him. Before we learned that Jesse understood the world differently, or to be more precise, *didn't* understand the world, we would get very frustrated with him over some things. I am sure we also frustrated him a lot more than necessary too. A huge amount of guilt started filling up inside of me when I realized all the horrible things we had done, not knowing. When he was close to the age of four he started having bathroom accidents almost every single day and we just could not understand why! We took him to many doctors and nothing was working. This went on for years and we worried that it would never end. We would ask him why he would not go to the bathroom and he would say he didn't need to. We would just look at him in total bafflement. Jesse had actually been my easiest child to potty train. He received more spankings and loss of privileges than I ever want to remember. I wish so much that I could take that all back now knowing that it was not his fault.

It was much later that I found out that gastrointestinal problems are another common marker of ASD. In fact, some doctors believe that is where the problem begins. Dr. Bryan Jepson's book: *Changing the Course of Autism* explains very thoroughly the connection of gut problems to the brain. Children with ASD have leaky gut syndrome because of intestinal problems that parents rarely know about or know how to cure. There are some very successful diets that are known to make a huge difference in these children's lives. I did not know about Jesse's AS, or his intestinal problems (even though, once again, we had taken him to doctors) until he was thirteen, so it was basically too late for us in the diet realm. How do you convince a teenager to stay out of the hamburger and pizza lines in the school cafeteria? And having him take a home lunch was unheard of in his opinion. By this time those issues had thankfully worked themselves out anyway. I do try to have some control over what he eats at home though. I have read that these diets may also help with other issues of AS such as cognitive abilities. If you are still in control of your child's eating then you may want to learn about these diets and see if they can benefit your particular child. You can find information on the internet or hopefully from your child's doctor. Keep in contact with his doctor to make sure your child stays healthy and gets the nutrition he needs. Many parents have had a lot of success with the Gluten & Casein free diet. It is a hard diet to follow but it may make a substantial difference in your child's life.

Every parent of a disabled child feels tremendous guilt. All we want is for our children to have what everyone else has and to be happy. I even feel wrong in using the word disabled when referring to Jesse because he is in fact *extremely able!* That is why I did not catch on that anything was different about him for so long. Most people that know him do not even know he has AS, they just assume he is really shy. After really getting to know Jesse and spending a lot of time with him, I am sure most of his friends notice he is a little quirky, but I do not think they know he has AS. I asked the mother of one of his friends if her son has ever said anything about Jesse being different and she said her son says, "Oh no, that's just Jesse." My nephew, who is Jesse's age, even chastised his mother (my sister) for "judging people" when she asked him if he ever noticed anything different about Jesse.

Jesse puts a lot of effort into not bringing attention to himself and just blending in. He is very well behaved and has learned that by copying people he can model his way through life as a total ordinary person. That is actually one of the things that makes him better than average. Jesse has taught himself, with no help from therapists, doctors or anyone, how to fit into this world that makes no sense to him. He does everything every other boy his age does, and more. He plays sports, goes to movies and hangs out with friends, asks girls to school dances (and they ask him), participates in church activities and scout camps, drives (his own car he paid for), has a job where they value him, does well in school, cooks, goes to boy/girl parties, and plays the piano exceptionally well. We are actually very lucky because he is the almost perfect teenager! He still has mood swings, but he is very obedient. He never argues, unless he is doing it in a playful way to show how smart he is. He just has a "look" when he is not happy about what is being said or done. But then don't all teenagers have "that look"?

Something that I have tremendous guilt over resulting from not knowing sooner is the fighting he and his dad would do. Bob did not know that Jesse doesn't understand and hear things the same way we do and he would get really upset with him when it looked like Jesse was not cooperating or listening. That would make things much worse because a child with AS **cannot** handle being yelled at. Nobody likes to be yelled at, but I have read that it can be extremely terrifying and upsetting to an AS child. I have seen firsthand the truthfulness of that. They do not appear to be able to pause and think of alternative strategies to resolve the situation when they are upset. There can be an instantaneous physical response without careful thought that can involve "blind rage" and not seeing the signal when it would be vital to stop.

There was one incident when Jesse was about twelve years old and he and his brother and sister were supposed to be helping their dad clean out our pool to put it away for the winter. R.J. and Tonisha were doing what they could see needed to be done but Jesse was just standing there watching. I am sure he was very confused and wanted to help but did not have any idea how. His dad, who was already not happy about having to clean the pool, thought Jesse was just being lazy so he yelled at him to get over there and help! Next thing I knew, they were in a fist fight! Jesse is not a weak kid, and he could really hurt you if he swung at you. Of course not too many fathers would stand for that. There were a couple of incidents like this one until his dad learned of his AS. Ever since Bob learned how he needs to handle things with Jesse and started to understand him more they have been best buddies. Bob is now really patient and considerate with him. And Jesse is very helpful and cooperative when he knows what is expected of him.

Intellectually, the child with AS has the ability to recognize his or her social isolation but lacks the skills needed to achieve success in that area. Parents have to provide the necessary level of guidance and encouragement to help their child. The child most often desperately wants to be included but just does not know on his own what to do. There hasn't been a single episode like the pool one since we learned about AS. If we ask Jesse to do something and very patiently show him how or continue to guide him through it, he is very willing to help and do anything for us.

It is a good thing we know about his AS now so that we can understand him better and help him more, but I do believe Jesse would have made a nice life for himself either way.

Bob and I have had the past six years, and many more to come, to learn about and experience "Holland" and it has, for the most part, been truly rewarding. We probably worry a little more and have different concerns than if Jesse did not have AS, but he has brought a lot of joy and understanding into our home.

CHAPTER TWO

What is Asperger's?

If you asked a person who has Asperger's what it is like to have it, they would not be able to answer that question. They do not know what it is like not to have it. They are just who they are.

Tony Atwood, the very well recognized clinical psychologist specializing in the field of Asperger's Syndrome explains it this way: "The brain is wired differently, not defectively. The child on the spectrum prioritizes the pursuit of knowledge, perfection, truth and the understanding of the physical world above feelings and interpersonal experiences. This can lead to valued talents, but also to vulnerabilities in the social world."

It would be nearly impossible to explain AS without including the whole autism spectrum disorder. The term Pervasive Developmental Disorder, or PDD, is the official category under which Asperger's syndrome is diagnosed. There are five PDD's three of which—Asperger's, Autistic Disorder, and Pervasive Development Disorder-not otherwise specified (PDD-NOS) are often thought of as being part of the autism spectrum and are commonly grouped together as autism spectrum disorders (ASD's). However, some believe that the term ASD only applies to autism. The two other PDD's, Rhett's disorder and childhood disintegrative disorder, are not always referred to as ASD's, even though they may have autistic behaviors.

When comparing autistic disorder, AS and PDD-NOS, the idea of an autism spectrum that links them seems logical because they all share a triad of impairments. All people with ASD have problems with 3 core areas of development: social interaction, verbal and nonverbal communication, and the presence of restricted or repetitive patterns of behavior and interests. However, there is a very wide range in the symptoms, behaviors and severity of each condition. Someone with AS may have a very high IQ and be above grade level in terms of academics yet have repetitive behaviors or feel compelled to engage in behaviors such as rocking that are more commonly seen in children with autism. The main differences that distinguish one PDD from another are factors such as age at onset of symptoms; severity of symptoms; combinations of symptoms; and the presence of other traits, skills or characteristics.

People with AS do not hear the same way other people do. They only hear limited parts of our sentence and therefore much of the time really has no idea what you are saying. It is not that they tune us out; they just sometimes cannot process that much at once. They also cannot read facial expressions or distinguish what our tones mean, which makes it all even more complicated for them. Even when they do understand what you said, they still have a hard time knowing how to answer a lot of the time. I explain this more in subsequent chapters.

A very large part of having ASD is always having to differentiate between someone being friendly or someone making fun of them, or being angry with them. This is because of their hard time understanding gestures, facial expressions and tones of voice. I felt really badly one afternoon when I asked Jesse to do me a favor and take care of our dogs. We let our dogs out of their dog run each afternoon to run and get some attention from us and I didn't have time to do it that day so I asked him if he would. He was very willing and happy to do it. Jesse was doing way more than I even expected by playing catch with them, running with them and just giving them a lot of attention. It made me happy to see the huge smile on his face knowing that he was having fun and was proud to be helping me out also. Everything was great until we realized that we had left a gate open and one of the dogs ran off. Bob and I were getting ready to go to an appointment so we didn't have time to go chase him down. Bob was really irritated and angry at the dog and he went outside and yelled *to* Jesse, "Go get that dumb dog!" Jesse took it more as Bob yelling *at* him and being annoyed with *him*. He looked crushed. Just moments before he was happy and helpful and now, in his eyes, we were mad at him and he was getting yelled at. We have to be very careful with what and how we say things to Jesse.

Along with not knowing what other people's intentions are, they also do not often know the proper way to respond to other people's feelings. To those who do not know about ASD's, these children and adults can sometimes seem uncaring. Most people with ASD actually have very deep feelings. It is all just very confusing to them. Jesse had a friend in junior high that lost his father in an automobile accident and the whole school knew about it and was trying to be sympathetic. I don't know how Jesse acted at school, but I can imagine. When he came home that day I brought it up with him to see if he even understood what had just happened. I told him how his friend was probably very sad and Jesse needed to show he cared. Jesse smiled cheerfully then walked off to his room.

Jesse is the sweetest kid I know, and he would never dream of hurting anyone. I just really wish I knew a way to help him understand people and know how to show concern and compassion. I always worried that this would be the one thing that could possibly keep him from being married someday. And then Bob gave me the sweetest gift of hope. We were driving home from my brothers' house one evening and talking about our kids when he said, "I'm sure Jesse will get married. It will be a really special person." His sister Tonisha believes he will too. He is only nineteen and I choose to believe he will also. Although Jesse does not show compassion in the traditional ways, people do always feel loved and accepted around him.

Some kids with ASD will manage it by imitating other people. Jesse has become very proficient through observing and mimicking other kids. He has learned what is appropriate in public and what he needs to do in the privacy of his home. He is overly cautious not to make a spectacle of himself in public. For example, many people with autism or AS have at least one self stimulating behavior such as hand flapping, hair twisting, spinning objects etcetera. We hardly ever saw Jesse do any at home or in public but we would catch him in his bedroom sometimes. He does play with his nose in the evenings when he is relaxing, which can be very annoying to watch, but we try not to stop him because he should be accepted in his own home. He also knows he needs to "act his age" in public but he can be silly at home. Can't we all? Through watching other people, especially his own age, he has taught himself how to act in different situations. With AS it is rarely a problem that they "just don't get it". They absolutely do. They have feelings and ideas just like anyone. The issue is that they have a hard time knowing *how* to react to things or to express their thoughts or feelings. And very often they do not have the natural instincts that typical people do not even have to think about.

Following is a list of some of the questions doctors use to diagnose ASD. If you have reason for concern and your child has more than three of these characteristics, they should probably be evaluated.

*Does the child appear unaware of social conventions or codes of conduct?

*Does the child have an unusual tone of voice?

*When talking to the child does he or she appear completely uninterested in your side of the conversation?

*Does the child give you very little eye contact? Or, tend to stare?

*Is the child's speech over-precise or pedantic?

*Does the child have an exceptional long-term memory?

*Is the child fascinated by a particular topic or topics?

*Does the child often become upset in changes of routines?

*Does the child have poor motor coordination?

Other examples that may cause concern may not always signify ASD but should be checked into, especially when there are two or more of the following:

*Remaining aloof, preferring to be alone.

*Difficulty interacting with others and failure to make friends.

*Not wanting to cuddle or be cuddled as a young child.

*Lack of social play (does not interact in make believe or group play).

*Does not respond to verbal cues (seems as if deaf).

*Difficulty in expressing needs or wants.

*Repetitive body movements (rocking, spinning, hand flapping)

*Aggressive or self-injurious behavior.

*Extreme and frequent tantrums.

*Short attention span.

*Over or under sensitivity to pain.

*Abnormalities in eating or sleeping.

*No apparent fear of dangerous situations (such as flinging self off the kitchen table or walking up to a ferociously barking dog).

A child with ASD may fail to respond to their name and often avoid eye contact with other people. They may also appear to develop normally and then withdraw and become indifferent to social engagement. Many children with ASD may engage in self-abusive behaviors such as biting or head banging. Some people with ASD become outwardly anxious or they may become depressed in response to the realization of their problems.

Most people with AS will at some point decide to try to "make it" in the alien world of typicals by finding some way to learn the rules and develop the necessary skills and coping mechanisms. Imitation of typical people is a major strategy to accomplish this goal.

Contrary to popular belief, children with AS *can* develop imaginative play. It is generally as a solitary activity. Jesse often made armies using Lincoln Logs as the soldiers and then had them bomb each other and the buildings he created. This was a very imaginative and acceptable form of play for that age I am sure, but he was much more comfortable and content doing it alone while many children would enjoy having someone to play with.

People with AS tend to take everything literally. This is why we need to deal with them logically and without emotion. If you tell a child with AS to "hold their horses" they are going to think you have lost your mind. What horses? And how would I hold them? How could it possibly "rain cats and dogs"? If you tell your child "We are leaving now," you better not mean after you change your clothes, empty and re-load the dishwasher and look for your keys. When *they* say it is time to go, *they* do mean that it is time to go! It is not a matter of letting your child run the family, it is a matter of respecting that he has had as much as he can handle and he is doing all he can to prevent a meltdown. They can only handle crowds for a short time (if at all) because it is so draining for them to "act normal". They are totally out of their comfort zone. And, if there are a lot of noises, sights, or smells, they may very likely have sensory overload. (I talk much more about this further in the chapter). I have noticed that as Jesse has moved into his teen years he has done very well with crowds and social gatherings. He finds somewhere to stand or sit out of the way, and just quietly observes everyone. He is always smiling and friendly.

Unique Skills of Asperger's:

Individuals with AS each have within themselves a spectrum of abilities and challenges. This section focuses on the abilities. The term "high functioning" is often applied to AS because people with this diagnosis typically have a normal or above average IQ and most exhibit exceptional skill or talent in a particular area, which is often their area of special interest. I believe that every one of us has at least one special gift or talent. The difference between typical people and someone with AS is that while many of us will obsess over our talent or special interest, we don't *need* it as dramatically as someone with AS may need theirs. It is an absolute comfort and aid to them in their chaotic world. Another difference is that even though we all have gifts and talents, most often people with AS are surprisingly skilled at theirs without a lot of instruction or preparation. Many are savants (a gifted or scholarly person) in that particular area.

Jesse's foremost gift is his music, and finding this talent has been very beneficial to him. Jesse, as with most people with AS, uses his talent to escape his confusing world and find peace of mind. He also does it for pure enjoyment. The talents and special interests (which are often one in the same) are a life saver to people with AS. They know they are successful at it and do not have to compete or worry about "doing it right". This is the one thing that they can truly enjoy and be themselves when engaged in.

What makes Jesse's gift of pianist especially interesting is that he did not want anything to do with the piano in the beginning…It is fortunate that he even found this gift. We bought a piano for me when Jesse was about eight. I took lessons for a year or so and got frustrated and gave up. Then R.J. decided he wanted to take them. He took them for a few months then quit. Next Tonisha gave it a shot and was not interested either. Finally, when Jesse was about age eleven, I suggested that he take a turn at lessons. He had no desire at all to do that. I begged and bribed him to just try it for a couple of months and see what he thought. We had no idea what was to come from that. Jesse only had one year of lessons at age eleven and now at nineteen is playing anything and everything he can get his hands on! It has been like that from the beginning.

Most people with AS will spend countless hours engaged in their special talent or interest. We were never the parents that had to push their child to practice piano; we are the parents that have to force him to *stop* playing piano when needed! Jesse will come home and walk straight through the door directly to the piano where he will play until dinner, bedtime, or something else stops him. We do ask him to play it for us often and he knows we truly admire his ability, but we try to steer him toward other interests also. Bob and I cannot even find sheet music that will challenge him anymore. All Jesse ever wants for Christmas is more music books. One year for his birthday I got a tiny bit more creative and took all of his piano books to be spiral bound so he could hold them open easier. He acted as thrilled as if it was a new car! (o.k., maybe not)...but he *was* very appreciative. We even got him a nice keyboard for his own bedroom so that when *our* desire of listening to the piano ends before *his* desire of playing it, he could accommodate everyone. He plays his own creations too, which are very nice to listen to, but he will not write them down. Jesse has a gift and we are very fortunate he found it. Playing the piano is therapy for him. It relaxes him and builds his self esteem. Whatever it is that your child with AS is gifted with, encourage him to share it with you. Showing your admiration of their talent is one of the greatest self-confidence boosters for a child.

Musical abilities are often one of the talents with which people with AS are blessed. Many are also truly skilled in mathematics, the arts, science, and the writing of fictional literature. I sometimes wonder if some of the most successful writers (whether in film, song, or literature) may have AS. If your child has not found their gift yet, help them look for it. Only a small percentage of people with AS do not have a unique ability. Many have more than one.

Many people with AS are capable of remarkable feats of memory and concentration. You may recall how Rain Man, from the movie with the same name, memorized every name and number in the phone book from A through G in one evening. He would be considered a savant, which is not as common, but almost all people with AS have some skill in remembering or memorizing things. I am always amazed at how easy it is for Jesse to do this. I wrote a four-page talk for him when he was about age twelve to give at church and he only had two days to prepare. The day he gave it he had the whole thing memorized!

An excellent memory is generally a good trait to have, but in some instances it is not. In Jesse's case it served him well while in school because if he was taught something even one time he would remember it. What has always bothered me, though, is that he may remember things from his early childhood that I would rather he forgot, such as us punishing him when he did not understand why, and therefore probably did not deserve it. (I will always have guilt for that even though we didn't know about his AS then). I don't even know if his elementary school years where enjoyable or not since he kept so much to himself and we could not "read" him. If he was teased or picked on when younger I would sure hope he does not still think about those days and let it cause him confusion or unhappiness.

Communication:

Young children with AS have early language development that ranges from normal to precocious. This is the opposite for children with autistic disorder or PDD-NOS, who may completely fail to acquire language or who acquire a number of words and communicative behaviors that seem to fade or disappear sometime around the second birthday.

Probably part of the reason we did not realize Jesse had ASD was because he never had a problem with language. He developed it at the normal rate and he did not ever lose it. He is never the one to start a conversation, but he will always answer as courteously and completely as he can when someone talks to him. Those with high-functioning Autism, or

Asperger's Syndrome, have relatively well-developed language abilities. They can speak fluently, in full sentences with few or no grammatical errors. Yet they most likely exhibit some difficulty using language in a social manner to exchange ideas and information with others.

Most of us instinctively know that it is not what you say but how you say it that fully communicates what you mean. Because people with AS lack the ability to interpret and use nonverbal forms of social communication, they often appear socially naïve or inept.

Many people with AS do very well speaking to a large group or audience. In that setting they do not have to deal with other people's body language and non-verbal styles. Small group conversations are very stressful. With one-on-one conversation you have to follow conversation transitions, facial expressions, posture or body movements, and keeping up with meanings and dialogue. These are all very complicated tasks for the person with AS.

Jesse is actually an amazing speaker when talking to an audience, which would surprise most people who know him since he doesn't talk a lot in general. When he has time to think and prepare something, he is very informative and entertaining. He looks at the audience, speaks relatively clearly and loudly, and does not even appear to be nervous. He also includes his great sense of humor and keeps things interesting.

There are many famous figures thought to have had autism or Asperger's who were insensitive to the subtleties of human expression, not knowing honest expression from sarcasm or humor from truth. They also were not able to read body or facial expressions. All were very intelligent in their field, explaining their recognition and appreciation in society. Just a very small example of these icons would include Albert

Einstein, Henry Ford, Vincent Van Gogh, Isaac Newton, and Ludwig Van Beethoven. Many, if not all, preferred solitude because of the difficulties they had with communicating and socializing.

One of the interesting language abilities of people with AS is that they may have a hard time explaining an event by talking about it face to face, but they show eloquence and insight expressing their inner thoughts and emotions by writing their account. Their written language is often superior to their spoken one, as in the following essay Jesse wrote for school.

The Food Storage Room

An essay by Jesse Harmon (age 13)

When my mom tells me to go get a can of pineapple for a delicious pizza, I rise magnificent to the occasion. I leap down the stairs, blow through the cold white door, and skimmer to a halt, trying to find the string that turns on the light to the cold storage room.

My eyes find their way to the luminescent ruby light glaring at me from the snowy white freezer by the wall like a freaky friend from some other world. I swing my hand around in hopes of finding the string that pulls on the light but instead feel a powerful crunch on the back of my hand, then hear a shattering on the floor and I realize I had just knocked down a Christmas ornament. Oops!

Finally I find the string and yank it down hard and all the room is suddenly filled with light. I saw a mouse dart from the corner with a "how dare you disturb my darkness" attitude; a copper colored spider big enough to tear my head off in one quick, swift motion, and the shattered glass of the Christmas ornament. I walked through to the other part of the storage room to find the pineapple. A freaky Halloween mask leaped out at me from the wall. I jumped three miles high with my face milky white from terror and backed into the rolling shelf's my dad had made. I spun around, clambering for a big, cold can of pineapple. I found one, snatched it up, and, keeping it close to my chest, sprinted out, thundering through the door and up the stairs.

Pretty descriptive for a thirteen year old boy who hardly speaks out load. Jesse has always been an expressive writer and when I am fortunate enough to find something that he has written it lets me see into his thoughts a little more than I would ever be allowed. I have always been envious of his school teachers because they assign him written work expressing his feelings and thoughts, which gives them opportunities to "know" him. I found a school paper in his room one day that was from his first day of high school and I cherished it because it was the only bit of information I would ever get about his experience. He had to write a short essay about that first day. Jesse wrote how he ended up in the wrong class room but didn't mind because by the time he realized he was in the wrong place it was the middle of class so he just stayed there. Nobody knew the difference. He also wrote that it was o.k. that it took forever to find his new classes because all the sophomores looked as lost as he did and he actually enjoyed being able to walk around longer. These are things he would never tell me. In fact, he didn't tell me *anything* about his first day of high school.

It is very common for people with AS to ramble on and on about their interests to the point of boring the listener. For the past eight years or so I had been confused about the fact that Jesse did not do that; he barely talked at all. When talking to a friend recently, whose grandson has AS, she asked me if Jesse was *ever* a "chatterbox" and, surprisingly, it reminded me that he was! When he was a young child I do not remember *what* he was always talking about, but I do remember that he *was* always talking! I remember us always telling him to quiet down. My friend was wise enough to make me realize that Jesse probably started to recognize that he was *doing something wrong* with his constant talking, since we kept telling him to stop, but didn't understand what and so he started doing the exact opposite by hardly talking at all. That is actually pretty amazing that he would even catch on that anything was "wrong" since most people with AS who have that characteristic do not ever become aware. Jesse didn't *completely* stop talking at that point, but he basically only did it when necessary. We never noticed a drastic change, but over the years we realized more and more how quiet he was, to the point of almost forgetting that he was not always that way.

Jesse went many years talking only when he had to. I cannot imagine how confusing it had to of been to him when people started harassing him for *not* talking after all that time of telling him to hush. Now as a young adult he has started to join in simple conversations with us when we initiate it. He has even just recently started offering up tiny bits of information about his day without any prompting at all from us. He never did that in the past. Jesse never did pick back up on his childhood rambling about one topic so I am hoping his years of "silence" at least taught him what is socially acceptable and what is not.

I can see Jesse putting a lot of effort into being more social as he gets older and it gives me so much hope that he will be just fine on his own. He also makes a real effort now to look us in the eye when we are talking to him, no matter how uncomfortable it is. It does not last real long, but he does it. Many people with ASD will either totally avoid eye contact or do the opposite, stare too intensely and for too long.

Most of the dialogue we have with Jesse is still a lot of joking around, on his part or ours. We also both take care of necessary business. It is just never too serious with Jesse unless we are trying to accomplish something essential. The important thing is that he is trying very hard to communicate much more than he ever has before. When someone with AS puts effort into two-way conversations we have to realize what an accomplishment that is and that they are progressing toward more social norms.

Those who have AS find other people very confusing. The main reason is that people do a lot of talking without using any words. For example, if you raise one eyebrow it can mean many different things. It can mean, "I think your kind of cute" or it could also mean, "I think what you just said was very stupid." The second reason they find people confusing is because people often talk using metaphors or similes, probably more than we realize. Imagine what the literal meaning of these phrases would look like in your mind:

> I laughed my head off!
> He was the apple of her eye.
> They had skeletons in their closet.
> The dog was stone dead.

Not very pleasant images are they? We can't assume that people with AS do not relate to others because they chose not to. We have to reason that they may just be hesitant to do something they find extremely difficult and problematic to them. Communication difficulties and the lack of implicit knowledge of social conventions and codes make the process of connecting with other people enormously costly in time and energy for the ASD person. The time taken to process social information is similar to the time it takes for someone who is learning a second language to process the speech of someone fluent in that language. If the native speaker talks too quickly, the other person can only understand a few fragments of what was said. It takes more time to process information through using intelligence rather than intuition, which is how people with AS have to do it. People with AS have considerable difficulty identifying and conceptualizing the thoughts of other people, and themselves. Sometimes it reminds me of the cute little dog tilting its head trying to figure out what its owner is saying.

A lot of the time with their concrete visual thinking and associative abilities, the imagery generated by some of our most common idioms and other figures of speech can be very disturbing. Even Jesse, who has caught on to a lot of it as he has gotten older still probably has no idea what we mean by things such as "Ants in your pants," "Butterflies in your stomach," or "Cat got your tongue?" These phrases can be very disturbing to some children on the spectrum. We have noses that run and feet that smell. How can a slim chance and a fat chance be the same, while a wise man and a wise guy are totally opposites? I never noticed how much we all talk like this until I paid attention to it one day. Go through just one day trying to count how many times you use this type of language and imagine how often a person with AS hears it in a day.

Conversation with a person with AS can include moments when there appears to be a breakdown in the communication. The person is deep in thought deciding what to say. This happens practically every time we talk with Jesse and it has taken me a really long time to train myself to give him the time he needs to respond before responding for him. Most people with AS have problems with auditory processing, which includes not always being able to process the entire sentence or question being asked. They may understand many of the words in the sentence, but they are not sure what to do with the information. They would most likely know the answer to what is being asked, but they have to first realize that they are being asked a question and therefore must answer. So, with things being taken literally, along with having hyper-acute hearing and difficulty with auditory processing, it is no wonder people with AS have such a hard time with communication. Of course I am talking about the ones who are even able to communicate at all.

A person with AS is also likely to avoid looking at the other person. Unfortunately, the temporary loss of conversation and eye contact can be confusing to the other person who expects an immediate answer or response and is unsure whether or not to interrupt the person with AS to resume the dialogue. But if the person with AS is interrupted in their thoughts, he has to start the whole thinking process all over again.

It is very difficult for even a very high functioning adult with AS to know exactly when to say something, when to ask for help, or when to remain quiet. Many people with AS appear to consider a conversation to be primarily an opportunity to exchange information, to learn or inform. If there is no practical information to exchange why bother talking? We see this in Jesse virtually every day. He will stand and look at me for a few minutes then finally blurt something out, as if he had to figure out if he should say it or not, or how to say it. Even simple things such as letting me know he is going to work early or that he wants me to wash something for him with my laundry. I have started teasing him a little when he comes and stands around for a few minutes and I know he has something to say. I will say comically, "May I help you?" He'll smile then tell me.

In Ellen Notbohms book: *Ten Things Every Child with ASD Wishes You Knew,* she has some very wise advice on learning to communicate with your child, which I feel is actually valuable with every child:

> "Start listening now to everything your child wants to tell you, including that which is not verbal. Look at him when he speaks to you, and answer him every time he speaks to you. Non response from him tells you: message undeliverable! Try a different way. Setting up the reciprocal exchange (he hears you, you hear him) gives him confidence in the value of his message, whatever it may be. That confidence will become the motivation that eventually moves him beyond concrete responses to spontaneous offerings, and finally, initiating thoughtful and thought filled conversation. That's a day all parents and teachers of language challenged children yearn for and dream about. While you are working on framing your communication in more concrete terms, be assured your child will give you lots of gentle, judgment-free direction to keep you on track."

Ms. Notbohm explained that perfectly and I could not agree with her more. I have been doing these things with Jesse for the past five or so years and I do see an improvement in his communication. It is thrilling to have him actually tell me something without me initiating it. He didn't previously do that and he does not do it often, but it is a beginning.

Although Jesse has began to talk a lot more again as he has gotten older, he does not have *deep* conversations. When he has friends over I will hear them goofing off and talking up a storm in his room, but it is not about anything meaningful. They are mostly just harassing each other about the game they are playing, or whatever else they are doing, and sometimes make a comment about another friend or someone at school. But maybe that is how all teenage boys socialize...I do not have a daughter with AS and I don't even personally know any females with it so I cannot say if they would be more socially perceptive or not. Interestingly, there are not even many books about girls with AS. We all know that *most* girls do love to talk about feelings and points of view though!

Jesse will talk to his sister when he is explaining to her how to do her algebra, or when he is making fun of her, like any older brother would, but never a serious conversation. He almost never starts a conversation but he will definitely state his opinion about something; he just won't have an in-depth discussion about it where you have much of a chance to reciprocate *your* opinion. I try to probe him to get more details and he will give me quick answers. One thing that has improved significantly in the past year or so is that he lets me know things such as if he is going to do something later with friends, or when he needs something. We are still trying to get him to understand that he should also tell us when he is leaving, instead of just disappearing all the time. He has a concrete schedule so we do always know where he went, but it is still odd that we will all be home and he just walks out the door without saying a word.

I try to be right there in the mornings to tell the children goodbye before they leave for school and Jesse seems to actually appreciate that, but if I wasn't standing there, and I didn't say it first, he would just walk out the door without saying anything. What is kind of special to me is being there to tell him goodbye when he leaves for work every afternoon. It has become part of his routine and I know he likes it. He will be sitting on the floor putting on his work boots and I will notice him even look at me before he gets up and walks out the door, as if he is making sure I get the chance to tell him goodbye. It is all part of the routine.

Your child with ASD only knows what has been directly taught to him through things such as school, books, movies, TV shows, the Internet, his experiences, and explicit instructions. He is genuinely not able to just sit in a room and understand social cues or how to "read between the lines" just through observation. Even as he grows up it is most likely he will not learn how to do this, he learns by facts. He does not "take in" what is happening around him that involves the rest of the world, only what directly impacts him. Many of the conversations he has had have been about knowledge and facts, not about feelings, opinions, and interactions.

Engaging your child in an ongoing language-rich environment is the surest way to build vocabulary and understanding. There is no pill or potion for instilling social capability. It builds upon itself, little by little, day by day. Communicating with a child with AS is a lot easier when we pause to consider our words. It may take some re-training, yours, not his.

It is important to say exactly what you mean and do not make your child figure out nonspecific instructions. Here are a few examples:

Do not say: Do say:
"Hang it over there."   "Hang your coat on the hook by the
                                                              door."

"Let's go."	"We are going home now."
"Your room is a mess."	"Please hang up your clothes and make your bed."
"It is too cold for that."	"Wear long pants instead of short ones today."
"I need my hammer."	"Please get my hammer from the tool box in the shed and bring it to me."

Typical children usually know what you mean with the simple phrases but many people with AS have a processing delay. When people speak to them they have to complete the following steps each time:

1. Receive the noise.
2. Filter out the background (they do not do that naturally like typical people do).
3. Hunt for hidden meanings or alternate meanings.
4. Formulate an answer, often by using sequential memory.
5. Reply.

Along with all of that they also sometimes make an attempt to translate the persons speaking tone or facial expression (which they have a very difficult time doing anyway) but are usually out of time and cannot complete it all fast enough for the expected answer.

Often boys who have AS do not ask questions about others or act interested at all about the other person's life; such as their opinions, feelings and experiences. They also have difficulty keeping a conversation going, especially when there aren't any questions being asked.

Theory of Mind:

As I have already mentioned, people with ASD have a hard time knowing what you mean just from the tone of your voice or expression on your face that would help typical people naturally understand. This is all part of theory of mind. Just yesterday this happened with Jesse and me. He was playing something incredibly beautiful on the piano that I had never heard him play before and I went and sat on the couch to enjoy it. When he finished I said, "Is that the first time you have played that piece?" and he turned to me, very offended, and said, "Well I'm just learning it." He thought I was noticing mistakes, expecting it to be better and saying it sounded bad! That totally threw me off and made me realize that there are probably many times a day that he misunderstands people. As Jesse has gotten older and lived through more experiences he has learned to recognize much more what people mean, but many things are still confusing or even ridiculous to him.

Many people with AS have a wonderful sense of humor. Jesse uses his quite often to let us know how silly we sound. For example, when Bob asked him if he was doing homework at the computer, when he could clearly see that he was, Jesse's answer was, "No, I just enjoy writing extra essays for my English teacher..." Or the afternoon his dad jokingly said, "I want the windows washed so clean that they don't even look like they are there." Jesse's reply was, "I'll just take them out." Jesse knew what Bob was saying but he decided to mess with him.

The OASIS GUIDE to ASPERGER SYNDROME by Patricia Romanowski Bashe, M.S. ED. And Barbara L. Kirby : Crown Publishers New York: pages 34,35 and 36 explains perfectly how people with Asperger's have theory of mind difficulty:

"To begin to understand what it's like to have AS, we need to consider what it means not to have AS. We pride ourselves on our individuality. Our society celebrates the individual, who does what he thinks is right, and who goes his own way. In truth, however, one sign of being neurologically typical is that we behave, think, and act in ways that are similar enough that, in most social situations, we have a fairly accurate idea of what to expect from others; we have a fairly accurate idea of what others expect from us; and we have the ability to say and do the things that will meet those expectations. One big advantage that a neurotypical person has over someone with a social disability like AS is that he moves through the world and relates to others with the understanding that others do have expectations of his behavior and a general idea of what those are. We're so good at this that we often meet the expectations of others even when we really don't want to. Some individuals with AS and other PDDs (Pervasive Development Disorders) don't understand why most people feel it's important to make small talk, dress in the current style, feign interest in people or topics they could not care less about, or tell white lies. If your friend asks "Do you like my new hair color?" someone with AS might reason that the friend really wants to know the truth. However, without even thinking, most of us instinctively "know" that our friend only wants—and only expects—to be told how flattering this particular "bozo-ish" shade of red is on her. So we do the socially appropriate thing and tell a white lie, which is not truthful, and yet not usually considered "wrong". This degree of moral ambiguity and rule bending that we accept as part of normal social interaction is unthinkable and can be quite confusing to a person with AS.

How did we learn when and how to tell this kind of lie? Moreover, how did we learn that it was not only okay to do but also the best thing to do? How did we learn to lie to our friend in this situation but not another? In less than a millisecond we knew to say "You look great." and our friend, who herself may have been thinking, I know this color was a mistake, replied "Thank you."

What accounts for this amazing ability? It provides the software that shapes the content and style of our conversation to fit perfectly the expectations of the other person to whom we are speaking. It automatically adjusts our body posture, gestures, volume and tone of voice, word choice and physical proximity. It alerts us to when we are being lied to, misled, pressured or embarrassed. Even more incredibly, it allows us to glean accurate information about things that weren't even specifically addressed in conversation, things that we'd have no other way of knowing. It allows us to have some knowledge of what other people are thinking; to predict in general terms and with pretty amazing accuracy what they will say and what they will do. It gives rise to having "funny feelings", "suspicions", "hunches", and "second thoughts" about a person or situation. It convinces us to take an action that in the moment seems irrational but "right": avoiding a particular stranger on the street for instance, or surprising a potential love interest with a meaningful look or kiss.

All of this is possible because most people possess "theory of mind", which is essentially the innate capacity to understand that other people can have desires, ideas and feelings different from our own. In addition, most of us have the innate ability to "read" nonverbal social cues, to naturally pay attention to what most of us consider the relevant information from our surroundings, and to instantly process all of that with little or no conscious thought. In contrast, people with AS lack or have an incomplete understanding of theory of mind. They do not know automatically and instantly what to expect or what is expected of them in social situations. Intelligence and disposition have nothing to do with our ability to read the minds of others. Despite a high IQ and a loving, generous disposition, a person with AS may still find themselves saying or doing the "wrong" thing, or even worse, not being able to defend himself against being deliberately misled by others or from being misunderstood. For now, however, it is important to understand that mind blindness is common to some degree in all ASD's. It lies at the heart of the disability AS entails and is often at the root of the behavioral challenges and social difficulties people with AS face."

I could not have explained that nearly as well and I would highly recommend anyone wanting to know *anything* about ASD's read this highly informative and well-written book.

It is frustrating knowing that your child with ASD has such a hard time with what comes so naturally to most of us socially, but that does not mean they cannot get by in the world. Jesse has learned so much through mimicking and studying the actions and conversation of other teenagers that he does not even seem to be having a hard time in the social realm, at least not to others. He has learned how to appear to be average. He even just recently taught himself to ask "What?" when he didn't hear or understand the question. He even asks for help with things once in a while when as recently as last year he would have never done that. Jesse has come a long way in giving more detail and having more confidence in his responses and conversations. He still almost never offers up information, but if we get him to talk about something he will sometimes chatter as much as anyone would.

Many children with ASD do not realize until they are in their teens that everyone has their own thoughts, plans, and points of view. They also think we all have the same beliefs, attitudes and emotions. They do not realize that everyone is not thinking the same way they are about a topic. This is part of their lack of theory of mind. With limited ability to *get inside your mind*, it is often difficult for a child with AS to demonstrate empathy for what you are feeling. A child with theory of mind problems might assume that since he is happy then you must be happy too. They also have a very difficult time with pragmatic language which is the ability to use language in a social setting such as knowing what is appropriate to say and when and where to say it. To be effective with pragmatic language you have to have theory of mind; the ability to figure out what the other person does or does not know and also what they may or may not want to hear. To help your child learn this concept you need to take every opportunity to explain how people feel in many different situations. Also help them understand why people would feel different than each other in the same situation. For example, if someone your child knows looses a parent due to death, divorce or any situation…explain why that person would feel much more upset than your child or even you would about the person leaving.

Typical people have the ability to understand others' feelings and know how to sympathize where most people with ASD do not. It is not that they are unfeeling, or insensitive, they just do not have that capability. Their brains are wired differently. Pointing out feeling situations in television shows and movies is a good way to create visual image to enhance their understanding.

There is a whole array of social actions and cues that most of us automatically learn that a child with ASD does not, and they can be very confusing. For example, we just know that it is etiquette to look at people when we talk to them or when they talk to us. We automatically know how close to stand next to someone, and how to read facial expressions. People with AS do not automatically have any of these impulses and can constantly slip-up.

Give your child countless opportunities to practice on you. Help him learn what certain facial expressions mean or different tones of voice. Ask him if he liked dinner or the shirt you bought him, and if he did not like it, teach him how to answer "the right way." Teach him what an acceptable distance to stand next to someone would be. The more we can teach them and help them understand, the more successful they can be when on their own.

Procrastination:

A trait that is very common in AS is procrastination. One reason could possibly be because they do not want to be wrong or mess up anything they do so they put it off out of the fear of not being perfect. Other times they may just not quite know what is expected and do not really know how to ask. We need to teach them that it is o.k. to say "I don't know" or "I need help". Many people with AS will not give those responses unless they are taught that it is totally acceptable and even common. Jesse actually says I don't know quite often now that he is older, but he will very rarely ask for help. It is not that he is too proud to ask for help, he just does not know how. I think a lot of the time it does not even occur to him that someone could help.

We are trying to help him with that by volunteering our help when we see he could use it. Jesse does always get what needs to be done accomplished, but nine out of ten times it will be at the very last minute. He is so responsible that it just does not seem to go hand in hand with procrastination.

Jesse decided to apply for Sterling Scholar in foreign languages his senior year. The very evening before his portfolio was due he got on the computer and started his resume and the other required forms. He did a great job with them, at the last minute, but then he came to me at 10:30 in the evening and asked if I had a folder and a paper clip. I didn't have either one and I was not about to drive to the store in my robe and slippers to get them. I guess I could have told him to go but then I would have been up all night waiting for him to get back and wondering if he was having a hard time finding the items, since that was not something he would usually buy. I found a folder that wasn't perfect but would have to do and told him to ask a teacher for a paper clip in the morning when he got to school. Luckily he did not get stressed out and upset (which is typical with AS) since things were not going perfectly to plan. Most people with AS are not very flexible and see only one right way of doing things.

Another time Jesse told me he needed 10 photos of things in our home for an assignment that was due in the morning, again quite late in the evening. I do not believe in rescuing our kids when they are not being responsible, but he just didn't get it. He did not see any problem with infringing on someone else's time frame. He is an excellent student and I have never had to tell him to do his homework, or even ask if he had any. I just need to teach him what inconvenience and impractical are. Luckily for him we were able to grab the digital camera, take the pictures and have our computer-savvy daughter, Tonisha, transfer them quickly and get them printed in no time at all. There have only been a couple of times his procrastination has caused real problems, such as when he tells us one hour before we need to be somewhere. I believe those situations are actually more of a communication problem than procrastinating though. If procrastination is Jesse's biggest fault, I guess we can learn to live with that.

Sensory Issues:

Sensory issues are very common with individuals who have AS. Ordinary sights, smells, sounds, touches and tastes of every day that we may not even notice can be downright painful for someone with AS.

Sound:

I remember when Jesse was only four or five years old how he would put his hands over his ears every time I vacuumed the floors. It actually irritated me that he did that because I thought he was being ridiculous. Remember, I had no idea he had AS or knew anything about his heightened senses. Only recently did I realize that he is not always hiding in his room to avoid the family, he is fleeing the piercing noises from the dishwasher, clothes washer, dryer, television and telephone all going at the same time! The other day my husband suddenly picked me up playfully to carry me off over his shoulder and I screamed to be put down. Boy did Jesse give me a disgusted look! He can't handle sudden loud noises, especially shrill ones.

Our auditory sense provides us with a tremendous amount of information and many individuals with ASD have hyper-acute hearing which can impair their hearing drastically. They may hear things too loud, too high pitched, too sudden, or just too much at the same time. Hypo-acute hearing impacts language and social learning, which is a main part of why people with ASD have such a hard time understanding and responding to social situations. As if that is not enough, with the added auditory processing problems, they are just not hearing the same way typical people are. It is not the least bit uncommon for a parent of a child on the spectrum to take them to get their hearing checked, especially before being diagnosed (we even did). And what is even more common is for the parent to be totally surprised when their child's hearing comes back as normal. Of course the way they seem to hear sometimes and at other times they are totally zoned out and not hearing at all just adds to the confusion before reaching a diagnosis of ASD.

I remember one afternoon when Jesse was about fourteen and he was just quietly sitting at the kitchen bar by himself in deep thought. I walked into the room, said his name and started talking about something. I probably talked for two or three minutes before I realized that he was not even noticing that I was in the room with him. I was not where he would see me since I was behind him, but surely I was making enough noise! That was one of the first realizations to me of how much was involved in having AS.

It is important for parent's and teacher's to be aware that most children with AS will have some auditory sensitivities and try to minimize them as much as possible. Sudden loud noises such as balloons popping, car alarms going off, screaming, thunder, power tools, the vacuum cleaner, dishwasher, hair dryer etc. etc. can actually cause physical as well as emotional pain to the person with AS who has heightened auditory senses. Basically the only thing you can do to shield your child from many of these is to supply him or her with silicone ear plugs that they can insert when a noise becomes intolerable. There is not a whole lot we can do about sudden noises that no one can prepare for such as a child's sudden scream. To understand how these sounds are to the person with AS compare it to the typical person who get's 'chills' hearing the chalk scratch the chalk board, or when a child has screamed right in your ear. The good news is that many children with sensory issues do learn to tolerate them much better as they enter adolescents and adulthood; though some people unfortunately do have to live with it their whole lives.

Clothing texture:

A sensory issue that many parents might not realize would be the different textures of clothing next to their child's skin. Even adults with an ASD often do not outgrow this one. A scratchy care tag in the sweater to you or I may be annoying, but to someone with AS it could be downright excruciating! I would imagine that anything made of wool would not even be an option, and to some even silk. I read of an instance where the child with AS insisted on wearing the same pair of sweats every single day and the mother had to wash them each night not only for cleanliness but out of fear that her son may start to prefer the unclean feeling or smell over the freshly washed one. I would imagine there are cases where it is next to impossible to keep a young child even dressed. This has nothing to do with stubbornness or trying to get their way. Many of the textures from clothing truly are impossible for some people with ASD to handle. Anyone who has ever had itchy hives or a bad sunburn and had to wear clothing that irritated it more would be able to appreciate what it may feel like to a person with AS to have this aggravation daily.

Taste:

Taste is a very complex sensory for people with ASD. We all have our likes and dislikes, of course, but there are some ASD children who would only include two or three items in their daily diet if allowed. One reason I absolutely believe that Jesse was not born with ASD is his drastic changes in diet. When he was a young toddler I would brag to everyone I met how my child would eat anything! There honestly was not anything he did not like. I did not even realize until he was about six or seven years old how that had changed. From that point on there was hardly anything he did like! We would get so frustrated with him and make him sit at the table for hours trying to force him to eat. Even now, at eighteen, he would still rather go without dinner than eat most pasta's, something with a sauce or gravy on it, or any kind of soup. Jesse can out eat anyone with hot dogs or hamburgers though! And he has always loved any kind of fruit. I do not cater to him very often, but if it is easy enough to just leave off the sauce, I will. Sometimes I will let him make a sandwich if I know dinner is something he absolutely cannot choke down. After all, the rest of us would love a bowl of clam chowder or plate of spaghetti once in a while. When Jesse was young, before we knew it really is a texture problem that would actually make him gag, we figured he was being ridiculously picky and we would not put up with it. He did a work sheet of self described definitions in second grade that I kept all these years because it made me laugh…and cry. For the word 'punishment' he wrote, 'when you don't eat your dinner and you have to sit there for over an hour by yourself.' I had huge guilt realizing this was many evenings of his childhood. (I include his whole list of definitions later in the book).

Visual:

The visual sense is most often the strongest in ASD children. This can be good and bad. They rely heavily on visual input to navigate their world, but it can also become over stimulating. They understand and have a much easier time digesting information when they can see or read it than just by hearing. On the other end, bright lights or too many objects can cause distortion and sensory chaos. Sometimes Jesse will just lie in the dark on his bed for long periods of time and I imagine it is not only relaxing but also necessary to overcome the days' exhaustion and confusion.

I read where a young man with AS describes how his brain is like a movie of his whole life. If he needs to refer to something happening at the moment he can quickly rewind to where that situation has happened before and see how it was handled. For example, if he witnessed a person lying on the floor at the school, or anywhere really, he could do a quick memory search of seeing that before (if he has) and know what to do by what happened the last time.

We all have memories and pictures in our heads, but the difference is that all the pictures in the memory of the AS individual are things that actually have happened. Other people have many thoughts and pictures of things that haven't actually happened. We may have a dream of the perfect place to live and the home we would like to own and what it would look like inside, but we have not actually seen it or been anywhere like that. Or we may envision our hair color and style totally different and picture what we may look like.

Sometimes typical people will say things such as, "If your father was still alive and here with you what would you say to him?" To somebody who has AS this is totally foolish. If your father is dead you cannot say anything to him. They can't envision the person being there and being able to talk to them after they are already gone because of course that has not happened. People with AS simply do not see any reason for "what ifs" because they are completely illogical.

Smell:

Many people with an ASD have a heightened sense of smell. This might also explain some of their food issues. Nobody wants to eat something that has an unfavorable or overwhelming smell. It is not always bad smells they notice though. They can appreciate a good smelling cologne, apple pie warming on the stove, a bouquet of flowers (usually), fresh air after rain. I am sure that someone with ASD has a much harder time than someone else might with someone who has not showered today or a baby that is overdue for a change. We all smell these things, but a lot of it we might not notice unless we are standing right next to the culprit.

Could you imagine how someone with ASD who has many heightened senses would feel in a grocery store? Bright fluorescent lights, many things to look at, muffled talking, crying babies, loud music over head, the fish at the meat counter is not fresh, someone is handing out sausage samples, they are mopping up a spill with ammonia...

One year for Christmas when my children were young I gave them each a little money and took the three of them to a small store to buy gifts for each other. I waited at the front of the store so they could surprise me also. After only a few minutes of being in the store, Tonisha and Jesse came to find me. Jesse looked pale and Tonisha informed me that he had just thrown up in an isle at the other end of the store. We went home and he was totally fine the rest of the day. Now, many years later, I realize that he had way too much to absorb and it made him nauseous. Whenever we ask him if he wants to go shopping with us he more often than not declines. If I do end up taking him I plan ahead on making it a quick trip. As he gets older he can handle a lot more than when he was a child.

Touch:

I saved this one for last because if it is not understood it can cause many problems, including hurt feelings. I always took it so personal that Jesse would wrestle around with his dad all the time and seem to enjoy it and he would let his sister punch him in the arm or even sit on him but if *I* came within a foot of him he would practically run as fast as he could! He did everything possible not to let me bump into him, leave alone hug or sit next to him. I only recently realized that he does not have a problem with *me* it is the softness of my touch he cannot handle. Many people with AS need to feel grounded and they do not like soft touches. It can be irritating and even painful to have someone give them a gentle hug or a soft pat on the shoulder. This could cause many problems in a marriage when the non-Asperger's spouse is not aware of their partners' soft touch anxiety. The good news, though, is that most people with AS who do not like soft touching really crave firm touching. My neighbor told me that her teenage son with AS loves when his dad will sit on him and give him the security of being "held down".

It is imperative for the main caregivers of people with ASD to acknowledge the different senses the person has a problem with and try to minimize them. It is not something the person with ASD can just ignore or put up with. Many of them are actually quite painful.

****

Time passes for everyone. Although it is likely your child's development will be uneven and he may not always seem to be keeping pace with his same age group, your child will mature intellectually, emotionally and socially. He will become more patient, more thoughtful, more responsible and more capable. He will become more independent and more grown up than he is today. There is no time limit on when he can acquire skills, abilities and understanding. Early intervention is not the only intervention. We are all capable of learning throughout our lifetimes. People with AS are no different.

Jesse has taught our family so much. He is so enjoyable and we are blessed to have a son with AS. He is probably one of the least demanding and most obedient teenagers on the planet. Of course my desire for Jesse is for him to have everything life has to offer, including marriage, children, job of his choice, friends and independence. But no matter what else happens or comes his way, the most important thing I want for him is to feel completely loved, admired and accepted.

CHAPTER THREE

Education/Therapy/Doctors/Specialists…

Many people with AS lead very normal lives and have never been diagnosed, or even care to be. They may feel a little "different" in the world but they get along quite well. There are many typical adults living and working right alongside someone with an ASD and don't even know it. There is really no reason for someone's AS to be spot lighted if that person can function appropriately and take care of himself. Others may benefit greatly from full disclosure in the work place. If it would help co-workers and acquaintances to understand them better and to know how to interact compassionately to their sometimes unconventional behavior, they would likely benefit from sharing their diagnosis.

I would not recommend to anyone not to get a diagnosis if it could help in some way because there is assistance for many situations, especially if your child is young and you have the financial means. You cannot get any services without an official diagnosis. After you do receive a diagnosis from a doctor you are still really on your own to find any kind of resources or help, but that is still the first step in qualifying for it. The help *is* out there and I would suggest your local schools be the first place you search. Unfortunately, any type of therapy is usually extremely expensive and insurances cover very little, if any. Public schools however are required to have special classes for disabled children.

It is not always wise to completely rely on the advice and direction of others, even when they are doctors or other specialists. As you learn more about AS you will also know more of who your child is and what their strengths and weaknesses are. You are the one who will know what works for him and what does not. You have to be your child's wholehearted supporter, specialist and advocate. You love him and know him better than anyone.

One thing I find very interesting when I am reading about different therapies that the experts are doing with these young children is that I had done many of these things naturally with Jesse, as any mother would with her toddler. By using common sense and trying to communicate with their children, parents end up unknowingly applying many of the same principles behind the established therapies being used. I had no idea Jesse had anything different about him, but of course I still spent many hours reading to him, playing with him, talking to him, and trying to get him to let me know what he wanted. I know one of the blessings for him and also me as his mother was that I quit my outside job when he was two and I was expecting my third baby . I chose to stay home to raise my three young children and do day care in our home. I believe that all the interaction he had with the day care children was in itself a real therapy for Jesse without me even realizing how necessary and helpful it was to him. Normally developing children can be excellent role models as the child with AS can learn by observing other children and see the desirable ways of acting and doing things that the others are doing. I did preschool, music, creative group play, story time, crafts and projects, outdoor activities and games, simple cooking and other things that I may not have put as much effort into if it had not been my job at the time. Jesse had a lot of interaction with many different children as well as his own mother at all times of the day. I also had a pretty stiff routine most of the time to keep things in order, which Jesse would have very much needed and appreciated. Children, as well as adults, with ASD generally depend on routine to give them some sense of control in their unstable world.

Jesse was cared for by my mom and my sister up until two years old while I worked outside the home, which was also a blessing. They both showered him with attention and very loving and understanding care. They read to him and R.J., took them to the park, let them color and paint, create with play dough, and many other naturally therapeutic activities. To us this was all just normal childhood activities. To Jesse it was all a crucial part of his growth and learning.

There are a lot of success stories where early intervention has helped young children with AS, especially those on the more severe end of the spectrum. But I do not think it should be viewed as a now or never opportunity for progress. I believe there should be more support for older individuals also. It might have made a lot of things easier for Jesse as a child if we would have known and gotten him help at a young age. However, he seems to be doing quite well on his own. His being "told" by being shuffled to therapist after therapist that he needed to be fixed all those years may have had a negative impact on him. And as I said, we did a lot of the therapeutic suggestions without even knowing that was what we were doing. Jesse was fortunate to be able to go throughout his childhood without a high strung mother hovering over him, which I would have been. He had the opportunity to develop who he is on his own and teach himself survival skills in his foreign world. Now at eighteen he is a very secure and confident teenage boy, and I give all of the credit to him for liking who he is and being determined to be happy and successful. He puts a lot of effort into being positive and having a "normal" life. Even though social situations are clearly uncomfortable for Jesse, he forces himself to participate and blend in.

Family doctors and pediatricians need to be educated on the therapies that lead to recovery from ASD. The AAP (American Academy of Pediatrics) has ignored these therapies for far too long. Pediatricians need to be able to get the parents started on the right track as soon as the child is diagnosed so that they have a chance of progression right from the beginning as we continue to search for more information. A lot of the therapies are things that parents can do at home. In the book *Son Rise; a novel by Barry Kaufman* about his son Raun, it tells their story of how Raun was recovered from autism through the dedication and immense therapy his own parents and family created for him. They used a method of love, acceptance, and understanding, along with teaching. Instead of trying to force Raun to come out of his world and be like them, they joined him in his world and slowly brought him out through teaching and acceptance. This family spent immeasurable hours working with Raun. They were also fortunate to have the means to hire help and also had many volunteers. But even if you are not able to hire help, what you are able to do in your own family will make some level of a difference in most cases. It is important to remember that you can get through to your child or teen with AS as long as you speak to them as unemotionally as possible. Make your message clear, logical and calm.

What I have learned from the many books I have read all comes down to basically two things: spend as much time as you possibly can with your child in an atmosphere of love and acceptance and teach them everything you can at optimal moments.

Dr. Temple Grandin is a successful and renowned animal scientist who is famous for her inventions of more humane and efficient cattle handling facilities. She has written many books, been the key note speaker at seminars across the country, and has accomplished many other recognized things in her life. She also has ASD. She describes her achievements by saying, "I developed my talent area. Often, we put too much emphasis on the disabled area. You have to focus on the skills you are good at and figure out how to use them to work around your disability." That is true for all of us.

Children with ASD who can learn their strengths and focus on them, developing them as they grow older, will have a foundation for future success.

In every situation that I have learned about where there is success or even recovery, it has been in part where the parents and everyone working with the child has let them be themselves while they are gently lead and taught. I take every opportunity I get to help my son understand something that society expects him to know. When he was young, even though I did not know about his AS, I knew that he needed to be taught some things that many people just do naturally. When he would talk on the phone he would just say "bye" without acknowledging what had just been said. I taught him that he needed to tell the person calling thank you for the information they called about; or if it was a friend asking him to come over he needed to say something like, "I'll be right over" or "I'll see you soon" or something similar instead of just saying a blunt "goodbye". He does much better now and actually has basically normal telephone conversations.

When Jesse was younger and still throwing major tantrums, even at the age of eight, I taught him to go to his room and pound on his pillow instead of trashing his room and destroying his things. I remember when he was in third grade and brought home a really neat picture he had painted at school. I could tell he put a lot of time into it and it was really nice. I was very impressed and I could see he was proud of it also. He had only been home for a couple of minutes when he got really upset about something and lost control, so I sent him to his room. I could hear him throwing things and tearing his room apart, which he did often, and when I went to inspect it later I found his picture torn to pieces. It hurt me, but it also hurt him. It was heart breaking to see how upset he was for destroying his picture in a moment of uncontrollable anger. That was when I taught him to use his pillow so he wouldn't do things he would regret, or hurt himself.

I am not trained to do any kind of professional therapy or help Jesse to fully understand the world, but I can help him a lot just by teaching him how to get by in it. I do everything I can to help him feel normal and like he is "doing it right". We want him to always know that we are proud of him and he does not have to be like anyone else. He just needs to be who *he* is. Every person with AS should be able to have that assurance.

One very therapeutic thing for Jesse was the quiet, peace and solitude he enjoyed while floating for hours in our pool. He would also spend hours at a time swimming under the water. I would compare it to being in a world completely his own for a while where he was sheltered from expectations and outside noise or interruptions. My neighbor's eleven year old son, who has AS, will spend many hours swinging really high. I imagine *that* is the quiet, peace and solitude he has found. I believe it is also a pleasant sensory experience in both cases for these two boys.

Many individuals with AS exhibit gaze avoidance and have difficulty making eye contact. They describe the process as painful, uncomfortable and even sometimes impossible. Many times when they do make eye contact they tend to either look too little or else stare. What I have realized just recently is that this can even change back and forth. Jesse always tended to avoid eye contact but within just this past year or so I have been noticing that now he tends to stare. But I have also observed that in the general public he seems to still avoid eye contact where at home with the family he does more of the staring. I wonder why that is. In addition to the sensory overload with making eye contact, they also may have trouble doing two things at once: looking at the person and listening to them at the same time. Even neurotypicals often have a hard time looking someone in the eye for very long. Many teachers have commented that even though some AS students do not look at them when they are speaking and giving instructions, the child still knows what to do, so they surely were listening and understanding. I feel that a child with AS should not be forced or expected to make eye contact when it is so stressful to them. Instead we could suggest to our child that they look at the chin or forehead of the person who is speaking to them instead of directly into the person's eyes.

I believe that the magnitude of help or "therapy" that your child needs should come right from you, at home, from the people who know him and love him most. Patience, understanding, and just plain kindness from all of us is what our children need to be able to learn and adjust to their foreign world.

CHAPTER FOUR

Asperger's Is Not Who He Is

Most people do not even know that there is anything different about Jesse. If they spend a lot of time with him they might notice some of his quirks, like how he does not always answer them, but they usually just assume he is really shy. Many people are really impressed with how happy and pleasant he is. Jesse has always been close to the perfect child; O.K, honestly, *after* we found out he has AS and understood how to deal with things around him he became the almost perfect child. It was always in him but he was not being treated the way *he* needed to be treated. It was his parents that needed changing, not him. I have had numerous teachers, neighbors, friends, relatives, and even strangers tell me how wonderful Jesse is. It takes a lot of effort for him to pull off his normalcy. He has to work extremely hard at the social stuff that most people take for granted.

Since we did not know about Jesse's AS sooner, we did not spend his child hood desperately searching for ways to "fix" him. We also did not over zealously try to protect him, which allowed Jesse to have a pretty normal childhood and have the same opportunities and experiences that other kids had. Jesse has always been a very likable and adorable kid. As a toddler he had huge, dark brown eyes and extremely light wavy hair. He has grown into a handsome, tall, physically fit young man with his hair finally turning a little darker and much curlier!

Jesse has always had friends and seemed to be included. I haven't heard of many situations where he was picked on, and I can only pray that when he was it only made him stronger. I believe that Jesse became aware at a very young age that he is different than his peers and taught himself in different ways how to succeed and blend into this foreign world he is living in. Jesse learned how to imitate those around him, even when what they were doing did not make sense to him.

If you spend enough time with two people who have AS you will find countless differences between them. If you spend enough time with one person with AS you will find a unique personality. Someone with their own likes and dislikes, their own temperament, and their own sense of humor. Jesse's sense of humor brings constant amusement to our home...except for maybe not to the person being teased. I was telling my husband Bob that our daughter Tonisha was walking around in her Prom dress feeling like Cinderella the other day and Jesse, who had just been told to take out the garbage, said to Tonisha, "Be Cinderella right now and take the garbage out."

Parents need to remember that ASD is something their child has, it is not *who* their child is. Once you find out they have ASD, it is easy to fall into the trap of thinking everything is associated with that. It starts to seem like AS (or whatever it may be) explains everything. However, never forget that there is more to your child that is due to who they are than to them being a person with AS.

Every child with ASD is born with his own personality, his own thoughts and feelings, his characteristics and traits and everything he is. Even if Jesse did not have AS I know he would still love every possible kind of candy! I know he would be very good with money and a hard worker. He would still enjoy reading, have a quick sense of humor, be very kind and respectful to others, love dogs, love any kind of fruit-especially kiwi, and have a long fuse before he explodes—just like his father. With or without AS he would be good at basketball, keep in good shape physically, love hiking and camping, and hate hunting and fishing-unlike his father. With or without AS Jesse would still have completed the whole 759 pages of Harry Potter all in one day. He would still be very faithful to his religion, obedient in school and at home, enjoy action movies, and going on long bike rides. He would eat like a horse, like every eighteen year old boy. And he would like girls, like almost every teenage boy. Jesse is and does all of these things because that is who he is.

We have to be careful not to blame, or give credit to the ASD for who our child is. Of course some things are characteristic of the disorder, such as how Jesse can move to any square on the Monopoly board without ever having to count, and he can add numbers in his head quite skillfully also. But I do not believe his physical endurance should be credited to AS. It amazes me how he can hike 20 miles or so without even tiring or ride his bike for miles and miles. Our kids are who they are…with or without their added ASD. And the good news is that most kids with AS really don't care if they are not like everyone else! They like their uniqueness and creativity. Jesse had to fill out some questionnaires about his AS recently and I was very pleased when I saw what he put. Even though he admitted to getting irritated easily and feeling lonely often, on any question that asked if he liked himself or if he was happy, he always put a resounding yes and always. He also put "always" on the question that asked if he enjoys his spare time. That illustrates that he is pretty content with his life and who he is, challenges and all.

Jesse has always gone to mainstream school because we never knew anything was wrong until he was in junior high and he always fit right in. His teachers have always loved him. He is the ideal student...respectful, self starter, hard working and kind to everyone. He has never had a difficult time learning. He gets along with the kids most of the time because he is kind to everyone. There was one instance in second grade when he was at recess and a classmate upset him so he just left the school and walked home without telling anyone. Luckily I was at home, but his teacher almost had a nervous breakdown trying to find him!

I am sure Jesse has never guessed that he has AS, and telling him was a hard decision we have struggled with for six years because we did not know if it would hurt or help him. (We did eventually tell him, which I talk about in the chapter 'Should You Tell Your Child They Have Asperger's?') Jesse has always known that he has a much more difficult time fitting in and knowing how to handle many situations than he should.

All that is awful or wonderful is not ASD. Our children have hopes, preferences, likes, dislikes, fears, dreams and interests like any other child. People with AS are interesting, funny, intelligent, handsome, friendly, honest, hard working, caring, generous, respectful, talented and dependable. How could any of that lead to unfavorable when discussing their differences from regular people? How perfect would the world be if *they* represented what was normal? Jesse does not judge or hurt anyone. He does not break laws or rules. He is not selfish or prideful. He treats everyone the same, with respect, no matter who they are or what they have done. I believe that Jesse's AS *is* a big part of him and gives him many exceptional qualities...but I also believe that it just adds to how remarkable he is regardless if he had AS or not.

When we had Jesse tested at his junior high school they had him take several written tests that showed he had a hard time with idioms, metaphors and similes but did very well on all of the academic sections. This is very typical of someone who has ASD and the specialist confirmed what I already knew when we were told he did have signs of Asperger's. But they said it was not bad enough to warrant any services or help. They did suggest that I get him involved in something at school or in the community to give him more social interaction. I had absolutely no idea what! Jesse's interests at that time were Stephen King and Dean Koontz novels, Lego's, Monopoly and dinosaurs! He liked to play chess but the junior high did not have a chess club. He was already on a church basketball team which he did really well on and enjoyed. What else was there? I decided to pray about it and my prayer was answered in a way I would have never imagined!

Jesse came home from school one day and said he was going to run for 8th grade Student Body Officer! This was my very introverted, quiet, 'shy' son. He did not even announce his news with a whole lot of enthusiasm, just matter of fact. I was shocked, to say the least. Jesse had never done anything so bold. He had always been more to himself and in his own little world that consisted mostly of being in his bedroom all day after school reading or doing something else quietly by himself. He didn't even spend time on the phone or with the radio blasting like most teenagers. He did play video games a lot which was typical, but usually alone. And he would hang out with friends when they initiated it. Now he was about to enter the world of popularity and being involved!

I was very excited, but also concerned, of course. He would have to communicate with a lot of people and be involved in new things he had never experienced before. Apparently a couple of his friends that he had had since elementary school were running and they told him he should too, so he did. And he made it! That was when I realized that he was very well liked and accepted at school. Most of the kids did not even see anything different about Jesse except that he was very quiet (they called it shy) and always had a huge smile. Friends and acceptance are what every mother wants for her child, even more so a mother of a child with any type of a disability.

Jesse's sister, Tonisha, even told us how popular Jesse was. It seems like from that day on, after deciding to run for student body officer, we couldn't go anywhere without girls coming up to him and saying hi. He just blushes, smiles and acts shy. He does not say much, just "hi", but his huge sweet smile says it all. He was even voted "most contagious smile" in the year book his first year of junior high.

Being a student body officer in the eighth grade was the best thing that could have happened to Jesse as a teenager who has AS. Throughout junior high and high school he was never short on friends. I know it makes him feel included and valued among his peers every time he and I are at a store and someone knows him and says hi, which is *every* time we are at a store! I even had a cashier ask me if I knew Jesse when I was grocery shopping alone once just because she recognized our last names were the same; and she hadn't even seen him since they were in junior high together. I would have never guessed things could have gone as well for him in that area. His father and I are so thankful that he has always fit in. That is a huge blessing for a child who has difficulties with socializing, which is the predominate challenge of AS. When Jesse was first starting junior high we were really worried that it would not be a good experience for him because of his social challenges and also all the changes in a totally different academic situation when compared to elementary where you are with the same kids and teacher all day. We had just barely realized that he had ASD, which brought so many concerns. His being accepted, in a much bigger way than we could have even wished for, was the greatest gift we could have ever hoped for.

Not all families have this great of a success story which is why it is so important to have outside help from kind and understanding neighbors and friends. Anyone that can show your child kindness and acceptance is very essential in their lives. Most children need at least one good reliable and sincere friend. As parents we can help our children with ASD who have a harder time making friends on their own. Initiate activities that your child can invite (or maybe you would need to do the inviting while they are young) other kids their age. Take a group swimming or to laser tag or just invite them over for pizza and movies. Do what your child enjoys and is successful at and invite other kids who you can trust will be understanding and kind to your child.

Try to get your teen to join a club or team of something they are good at. There they will find other kids with the same interests and friendships may develop over their shared talents and interests. Jesse has a very good friend who is also a gifted pianist and they support each other in that as well as hang out together at other places because they have things in common and enjoy each others' friendship.

Most children with ASD have a very hard time starting friendships on their own because of their social challenges, but they are very capable of having them. Being alone does not always mean that your child is lonely, they need this solitude. But they also need *some* interaction with others. Some people who have AS are perfectly content being alone while others desperately want friendships.

We are very fortunate to have moved to the town we did when Jesse was only in the fourth grade. We had no way of knowing then what a blessing that would be for him. It was a small, close knit farming community where everyone is related to each other. It was a totally new atmosphere for our family. We were living the only place I had lived so far where you had to stop your car to let ducks cross the road, or where you could glance out the kitchen window in time to see a bald Eagle soaring through the sky. The Roosters waking us up at the crack of dawn took some getting used to, but now I don't even notice them anymore. In the beginning, the kids and I would tease their Dad, an avid hunter, for giving us whiplash in the car every time he spotted a pheasant in one of the fields. I also made bets on which one of us would be the first to drive our car into one of the huge ditches that surround us everywhere. We are up to our fifth and last driver in the family and no accidents yet!

Our new residence had a lot to offer but the greatest thing was how accepting and friendly everyone was there. All of my kids were fortunate to find friends quickly, but Jesse hit the jackpot. There was a large group of kids his age in our neighborhood who were also in his church group and they were all amazing kids. Every one of them welcomed Jesse right in and a few of them became really good friends with him. Thanks to these boys he has been able to participate in everything a typical teenage boy would.

When Jesse asked a cute girl out on a combined date when he was sixteen without any help from anyone, all of his friends, as well as his parents, were very impressed. It was his first date. I cannot emphasize enough what an accomplishment this would be for someone with AS. We heard from the others that went (since Jesse isn't big on conversation) that it went really well. He asked another girl to his high school's Homecoming dance in eleventh grade where they went with a group and the week after that dance one of the other girls in the group asked Jesse to the next school dance!

Jesse really enjoys hanging out with friends and even in groups, but he does need his down time. After a long day at school or work he will almost always play the piano or go in his room to be alone and unwind for a while. Most people with AS need their solitude quite often to rejuvenate.

As much as Jesse loves piano, he does have other interests too, even though they are few. People with AS are usually very routine oriented. Jesse has a basic routine of piano, basketball, video games, reading then starting all over. If he does not have anything else he needs to do, like his job or something with the family or his friends, he will continually spend the day doing these things. He rarely sits around doing nothing. Up until he decided he was too old for it to be acceptable anymore he also loved Lego's and built some pretty impressive creations from his own imagination. He is also very interested in dinosaurs. Many kids with AS are. Ever since I can remember Jesse has loved them. He knows, can spell, and pronounce every name of every dinosaur and knows every fact about them also. We saw a news story about new dinosaur bones paleontologists dug up recently in southern Utah and Jesse was thoroughly appalled at how the newscaster was butchering the names of the dinosaurs! Jesse does very well in science and archeology subjects in school and I believe he will be a very successful paleontologist one day.

Recognizing and focusing on your child's strengths and unique gifts and encouraging others to do the same can go a very long way toward making up for his areas of difficulty. By taking advantage of the gifts associated with ASD and creatively using them we can produce natural solutions to would be problems. You are building your child's self-esteem, especially when others are acknowledging their gifts and talents also. People with ASD who are given many opportunities to succeed tend to adapt to the world more quickly and much better than those who are taught to view everything as one dilemma after another.

Basically, we have always tried to treat Jesse as if he does not have a disability at all. I do tend to baby him and worry about him and I teach him at every opportunity. We also know some things need to be handled a lot more delicately with him...but Jesse can do anything *he* thinks he can or wants to do. We do not ever inhibit him from trying something new because of our own fears. The only way to keep him perfectly safe from physical or emotional harm would be to lock him up in our house. That is actually what they did do in the 'olden days' with anyone who was different, but for much different reasons. People tried to hide their children who were autistic or anything associated with it. They were seen as crazy or schizophrenic and they were not accepted in public. That is not a life worth living. It is not even rational.

People try to tell me things Jesse will not be able to do because of his AS and I tell them that they do not know what they are talking about. I am always pleased when I get to prove them wrong. Most people generally mean well and think they are looking out for him, but I choose not to hold him back or deprive him of anything that is possible. He always amazes us at how independent and capable he is. There are the people in life who are given great hardships or challenges and they choose to excel and there are others who choose to wallow in self-pity and lose out on what could be theirs. Jesse belongs to the first group and nobody is going to take that away from him because of their own insecurities. We need to support and encourage people with physical or mental challenges, especially when they are our own children. I am not saying it is easy for them. Everything they do is considerably harder for them than most, but that just makes them even more proud and deserving of happiness every single time they achieve it.

Jesse does not even let his own fears slow him down like many of us do. I am sure he has to be terrified every time he is in a new social situation, but he doesn't let it show. He does more than is expected of him when other boys his age sometimes would not even do it. It's not even hard for *them* usually, they just don't want to.

Many people with AS have a lot of integrity and are people pleasers. If they are asked to do something, a lot of the time they will do it just to be helpful. If Jesse refuses to do something I know he is having great anxiety over it for one reason or another. I have learned through all these years of raising him that he will do anything that is asked of him unless he has a very good reason not to. A lot of the time it may be something he is just totally uncomfortable with or does not know how to carry out.

The youth in our church were involved in a very large production where singing and dancing was exhibited. There were over 3,000 adolescents participating and each one was needed. Jesse volunteered to be on the stage crew and went to all of the practices until one morning he suddenly informed me that he wasn't going anymore. He did not even seem to realize what a problem that would cause! I was really confused as to why he would just suddenly shirk his commitment to this since it was not like him to do that. I tried to make him realize how much people where counting on him now and that it was too late to just stop going. It did not matter what I said, he was not changing his mind. He wasn't defiant or argumentative, he even seemed apologetic. I finally got out of him what the problem was…he **was not** going to dance. When he first signed up there was no mention of the stage crew having to dance.

The first week that they informed Jesse that they wanted him to be in the final dance, everything took a turn for the worse. Performing is just not something he is comfortable doing, at all. It is not a matter of *won't*, it is a matter of *can't*. Most people with AS are not known for their gracefulness. Some are even downright clumsy. I do not know if that is Jesse's fear or it is just worrying about messing up in front of a lot of people; but whatever it is, I know it is a genuine anxiety for him.

Jesse takes part in everything he can that he sees society view as normal or expected. He plays basketball and other sports with his friends, cooks his own meals sometimes (as much as any teenager would), drives a car (his own car that he paid cash for after only three months of saving), is planning for and saving to go on a mission for his church, goes to work every day, plays video games, and listens to music. Jesse loves his independence and we are always amazed at how self-reliant he really is. He is very proud of himself when he does things on his own such as cashing his check for the first time, driving somewhere far and new, having a good job and his own money for things he wants and needs. He does not want to miss out on anything that everyone else gets to do, and we are not going to let him. Sometimes it is scary and uncertain, but we have to let him see what he is able to accomplish. So far it has been everything he has tried. Things seem to just work out for him. People with ASD like everyone else deserve the freedom to succeed. They have to work so much harder to do the things that others get to do, what right do *we* have to stop them?

A funny thing that happened recently proved to us how independent and capable Jesse really is and that we, his parents, could have been the cause of some major grief by trying to help too much. He was expected to go to a school function for one of his classes at a different high school one evening which was about 15 miles away. Jesse had never been to that school, or even that area. It was in a big city where he would have to drive on three very busy major roads to get to it. I had offered to go with him and shop while he attended the school function, but there was no way he was going to let that happen. He was very confident and insisted on going by himself. He did not even seem the least bit uncertain. So, being the good parents we are, we drew him a map and told him every detail down to every street to turn on and even what business would be on the corner of his most important turn. I did not find out until the next day after everything went very smoothly for him that we totally messed up! Luckily he had decided to Google the school and look up a map himself, which was a very good thing. We had told him the wrong street number to turn on and the business that we said would be a landmark was no longer there! If he would have relied on us instead of himself he would have been driving around that city lost, for maybe hours.

Many parents of a teen who has AS are very reluctant to let them drive. I was one of those parents. We worry that their reflexes are not quick enough or that if they get pulled over or have an accident they might not know how to react and could even lose their temper. We worry that their bad sense of direction will very often result in them getting lost. (*I* don't have AS and I do that! Jesse and I are quite the pair when we are trying to find somewhere new together.) We worry about a number of things related to driving. The truth is, many teens with AS drive very well because they obey the rules! When Jesse took the test to get his learners permit (before drivers education and only a few minutes with the study manual) he only missed 1 question. Many people with AS generally remember everything they learn, so teach them well and they should do well. Have your child carry a cell phone and a card that explains AS. If they get pulled over or in an accident teach them to give the card to the police officer. Also teach them to call you in those situations. Jesse has been driving for four years and has not had any interaction with the police yet. I would say that is a pretty good record for a new driver.

One of the hardest things for us as a parent, especially one with a disabled child, is to give our child permission to grow up and make their own life independent of ours. We have the responsibility as the person who loves them the most to build their self-esteem as a foundation for social and other risk taking, and also to help them build a shield against the unkindness of others. A child with ASD can achieve a lot when healthy self-esteem leads the way. Help them find what they are good at and encourage them to develop it and to be proud of who they are. Teach them what they need to know then give them chances to explore their world and try new things on their own, as long as it is within their range of abilities. Realize that their ability is probably a lot greater than we dare believe. You know your own child and you have to be fair to them as well as yourself on what risks you are willing to let them take. Remember they *have* an ASD; it is not overall who they are!

The only reason I would want Jesse cured from AS is if it made things easier for him. I would not want him to be any different than who he is. I read a phrase somewhere recently that was very humbling to me…"I asked God to make my disabled child whole. God said "No. His spirit is already whole, his body is only temporary." Enough said.

CHAPTER FIVE

Friends and Family

Jesse has had many good friends throughout his teenage years and they are all still kind to him. But one thing that really concerns a mother of a child with ASD is to see some of their child's close friendships start to suddenly disappear. Part of this is natural as kids get older and have different interests or get girlfriends/boyfriends and jobs to take up their time. We still can't help but worry that their friends have outgrown them or decided that they do not want to deal with the differences or odd behavior anymore. It is so hard to not take it personal. We desperately want our children to always have friends and it is scary to watch even one friendship fade away. All parents must feel this way with their children. Every time the phone rings and it is someone new inviting Jesse to a party or to hang out it is like Christmas, *to me*. I want him to be included and involved. Jesse has a group of four really close friends that all hang out together, but it is an added bonus when someone 'new' turns up also. Jesse has been very blessed to have always had so many really good friends.

One thing that really helps when your child or teen is having friends over is to have a plan of what they will do already in place. Structured activities work best for younger children with AS since it is not uncommon to find your six year old with AS off playing by themselves when friends are over. Having a specific idea of how to fill the time may also help your teen.

The AS teen will not just "hang out" and talk or listen to music like most teens are comfortable with doing. They also most likely will not have an idea of what they want to do when their friends get there. The friends will sometimes have ideas, but it saves a lot of awkwardness if you get your teen to think of something before they come. We have all heard, " What do you want to do?", "I don't know, what do *you* want to do" repeated over and over again. You can offer suggestions to your son or daughter ahead of time, or just get them to start thinking of options. The most critical rule, though, for the parent of a teen, *any* teen, is to have plenty of food on hand! If you have food, everything will be just fine. Whenever Jesse is going to a party I ask him if they will be eating there or if he is planning on eating with us first and his answer is always, "What are *we* having?" I should realize by now that he will always be eating at the party, he'll be eating *both* places if it's good! Just today he got invited to a party later tonight and I jokingly said, "So I guess you won't be eating here then" and he gave me a big grin and said, "But we are having lasagna..." Only a teenage boy could eat two whole dinners!

Jesse is hilarious, like many kids with AS are. He has a very enjoyable sense of humor and knows how to laugh at himself. It is very refreshing when someone knows how to laugh at themselves instead of becoming defensive when they mess up. One morning Jesse made pancakes for the family for breakfast and I wasn't paying any attention. When I sat down to eat some I noticed that R.J. and Tonisha, who had already started to eat, were acting a little reluctant about eating their pancakes. They were both slowly picking at them and seeming to even gag each bite down with plenty of milk. Neither of them would look at me. After I took my first bite I could taste what the problem was, Jesse had somehow mistaken baking soda for baking powder! They tasted awful! And what was really funny was that R.J. and Tonisha thought that *I* had made them and didn't dare say anything. We all laughed when we realized his mistake, including Jesse, and made a new batch which was much more edible.

Jesse is actually a very good cook. He likes to go to the grocery store and get all the ingredients he needs for refried bean burritos and invite a bunch of friends over to eat and watch videos. He even uses his own money to get the food and movies. I have to admit that his burritos are always much tastier than when I make them. He also loves mashed potatoes which is a bonus for me because I like to eat them but I don't like to peel them. He is more than willing to make them for us.

Jesse's sense of humor showed up the other evening while Bob and I were relaxing on the couch in the piano room listening to him play "Beethoven's Moonlight Sonata" which happens to be 17 pages. We were thoroughly enjoying our private little concert when Jesse suddenly just stopped playing right in the middle of the song, stood up, and just matter of fact said, "I have to go to the bathroom." He gave us a big grin and walked off. All three of us laughed so hard at the thought of how that would *never* happen at a real recital…even *if* the song was 17 pages!

Most people with AS take things very literally and Jesse is no different. Idioms, puns, nuances, metaphors and sarcasm are usually lost on people with ASD. Now that Jesse has caught on a little more that people don't always mean exactly what they are saying he is very funny! As he has gotten older he has learned how to put the illogical things we say into comical comebacks. One day Jesse told me he was mowing lawns for a scout activity and I laughed and said, "It sounded like you said you are rolling lamas." He smiled and said "We've been known to do that too."

His dad once said, "Don't open that can of worms," and Jesse responded with, "Why would I want to open a can of worms?" He doesn't say it to really want to know or necessarily be sarcastic; he says it to show how silly that sounds. I asked him to get his dad and me a drink and he said, "Just one?" and smiled. Two of his favorite things to say when his dad is being a pest and teasing him, which is quite often, is, "You are not behaving appropriately" or "You need to settle down." That always sounds funny coming from the child to the adult. Yesterday Bob was harassing Jesse by chasing him with a black magic marker saying, "I should color you in a mustache." Jesse said, "I should color *you* in one," and Bob replied that he already has a mustache and Jesse said, "But it isn't colored!" (Bob's mustache is quite grey!)

Jesse truly appreciates the little things that we all take for granted. Simple things such as telling him goodbye each morning before school, hot baths in a peaceful atmosphere, dessert before bed, playing with our dogs, getting something-*anything* new, a birthday card or gift, money he has earned, candy—always candy! The day after his high school graduation he was outside pulling weeds in our vegetable garden and I took some mail to him. He had received two congratulation cards along with some money from two of our neighbors who know him well. His grin could not have been bigger than if it would have been a thousand dollars. On the flip side, they could have just been simple pieces of note book paper saying good job and he would still have appreciated their thoughtfulness just as much. He jumped right up and went into the house to call them both and tell them thank you.

Jesse has a really sweet ritual he does every single day that I know his wife will really appreciate if he keeps it up...He always says, "That was good" right to me after every meal as he is cleaning up his plate. Even if I know it was not something he truly enjoyed I appreciate his little show of thanks for my efforts each day. Jesse has always treated everyone with kindness and respect, and he usually get's it in return.

As a young child Jesse would always put little gifts on our beds such as candy, a note, or one of his toys. One Christmas he must have been doing the 12 days of Christmas because I would find a sweet little note every day for over a week. As a child he was always so willing to do anything for anyone and do it happily and without expecting anything in return. As he has gotten older he tries to make bargains sometimes and is a little less willing, but that's a typical teenager isn't it?!

Jesse's letter to Santa at age seven:
Dear Santa
I want a bike and dinosaurs and cars, and a train set.
And to be nice.
Sincerely
Jesse

We can usually bribe Jesse to do anything with candy. He loves it! All of it. When the kids were young, the three of them took turns having our dog sleep in their bedroom at night. Every time it was Jesse's turn, Tonisha would offer him candy to let her have the dog. I would sometimes offer him candy (or a hamburger, which he also loves) to do yard work. I believe kids should help out at home anyway but if all I had to do was give him a hamburger or candy to have his assistance in the yard willingly and even pleasantly then it was totally worth it!

Unfortunately, there is one thing that I cannot bribe him to let me do...give him a hair cut! He will fight me like a badger and then avoid me the rest of the day if I even mention it. He goes into hiding. I finally realized that it is probably a very traumatic experience sensory wise. I am guessing that most people with ASD avoid getting haircuts. He is feeling the scissors tear through his hair, hearing them clicking so close to his ears, seeing his beloved hair drop to the floor, and feeling the anxiety of what the final outcome will be. He also has to put up with my standing so close 'in his space'. It is often very uncomfortable to have someone that near, especially with ASD. Not to mention the itchy hair landing on his neck and shoulders then falling down his back. Some people with ASD also have an obsessive compulsive disorder that may make it hard for them to actually give up a part of themselves such as their hair. Jesse, along with many people with ASD, does not like attention brought on him, which a new hair cut almost always inevitably does for anyone. This last time that he desperately needed it cut I got creative and it worked. I told him to think of something he wanted from me and we would make a deal. He wanted the foot pedal on the piano fixed. He watched as his dad fixed it, then he gave it a test run, then reluctantly stuck to our agreement.

Sometimes abuse sadly takes place in a family when parents just cannot take anymore. These parents need outlets and support for their child's sake as well as their own. They can find support groups by searching on the internet, asking around in their own communities, turning to friends and relatives, and checking with hospitals and religious affiliations. Parents need a way to distance themselves from their child when they are getting extremely frustrated or upset. It would be ideal to have a safe place in your home that you can leave your child alone for small amounts of time. This would allow you some distance when you need it before something drastic happens. If that is not possible, call someone for help before your patience is gone.

When Jesse was about eight months old I was at work one day and Bob, who was with our boys in the mornings before he went to work, called me. He was about to lose control. Jesse had been screaming for hours and Bob had done everything possible to calm him but nothing was working. I told him to put Jesse in his crib and then take R.J. and go outside for a little while where he could not hear Jesse. He did, but when he came back Jesse was still crying. He had fed him, changed him, held him and tried to comfort him...nothing worked. At his wits end, Bob ended up punching a hole in our hallway wall. I was actually very proud of him that day. A wall can be fixed.

It is pointless to ever try to force someone with ASD to do something. You will always loose. They absolutely will not do something they object to, no matter what you may threaten them with. And if you push, you will most likely cause a substantial battle between you and them. For one thing, you cannot force *anyone* to do something, and it will cause plenty more problems than if you get them to cooperate the "right way". There are so many better ways to get their compliance. People with AS are generally people pleasers. They want to follow rules and do what is expected of them. They like feeling useful and helpful. If you ask in the right tone and respect their time frame (do not ask when you can clearly see they are busy), give them plenty of notice, explain exactly what you need or want from them and explain why, then show them your appreciation, they will almost always comply. Jesse also likes to know how long it will take. All of us like these considerations. It sure doesn't hurt to let your child see that they are needed also. I always tell Jesse I need "his muscles" when I need his help moving something or lifting something for me.

Siblings often know well before the parents or other adults that their brother or sister is unusual and they may be compassionate and tolerant or they could be embarrassed and antagonistic. R.J. was the first one to ever notice there was something different about Jesse. They spent more time together than with anyone else. He never said anything though, until much later after we all realized that Jesse has AS. When they were both toddlers they got along great. R.J. was always making Jesse laugh and he would often get books and pretend to read to him which Jesse loved. They were always together. R.J. does not remember exactly when it happened, but it seemed like overnight that Jesse did not want to hang out with him anymore (sometime around age eight or nine). Every time R.J. would go into Jesse's room Jesse would yell at him to get out. R.J. tried continuously to play with his brother until after a couple years he finally became too frustrated over the rejections and basically gave up. I do not know if I will ever understand why they played together so well when they were younger and things changed so dramatically around this time. It was very upsetting for R.J. to lose his friendship with his brother this way. They never did gain the typical brotherly closeness many siblings have, but they did learn other ways to enjoy each other. As R.J. reached his teen years he developed a fun way of joking with and just being friendly with Jesse in a non-threatening way that Jesse also enjoyed. He can still make Jesse smile anytime he comes around. When Jesse was in second grade another student was picking on him after school and R.J. (who was in the 5th grade) went over and stood up for Jesse. That made me so proud. I know R.J. will always watch out for his brother.

Tonisha and Jesse treat each other like any other teenage siblings would. They both go around playfully punching each other in the arm, joking around and teasing each other. He helps her with her homework (sometimes she has to bribe him with candy) and she helps him with his look, insisting that he could straighten his tight curly hair if he really wanted to. She eats his mushrooms from dinner and he eats her potatoes. When they were young she would get him to come into her room and read to her for hours. She didn't want to be alone, so she would sit in his room and do her own thing all the time while he would do his. They hardly even noticed each other but they liked the company regardless. They most likely will never have deep conversations together, but they do have a close connection that works great for them. Tonisha understands Jesse and accepts and loves him for who he is. He has his ways of showing that he cares about her also.

Siblings of children with ASD or any other disability are often very caring and selfless individuals out of necessity. They sometimes take personal responsibility for their challenged sibling's happiness and acceptance. Often they have to take the back burner for parents' time and attention since the child with the disability requires so much. They also do not get to enjoy the typical relationship that common brothers and sisters share. But there are so many beneficial aspects for these kids. They learn patience, understanding, kindness, acceptance and gratitude. They have the aptitude to mature and learn more quickly how to put others first than most children in regular family settings. They also learn to appreciate differences and not tease or criticize what others have no control over. They can be very kind hearted, compassionate and giving people who may stand up for the little guy in many situations.

Many children with AS are brutally honest and speak their mind. Their allegiance is to truth not people. They often need to be taught why it is appropriate at different times to say something not true and at other times it is best to just keep quiet. For instance, when mom gets a new hair cut that turns out absolutely ridiculous...and *she* even regrets it, the last thing she wants to hear is her seven year old child telling her how awful she looks! Jesse actually does keep quiet most of the time, which is surprising because of how honest he naturally is. I will admit he has given me plenty of funny looks with some of *my* new hair styles though.

Jesse never informs adults when a peer has done something wrong, or in other words, he does not tattle. Even if I flat out ask him about a situation involving his brother or sister he won't say much. When he was about six years old and R.J. was eight, Jesse even took a punishment that should have been R.J.'s, because he kept quiet. We knew one of them had taken something from us and we questioned them relentlessly. As R.J. kept insisting it was not him, Jesse sat quiet. We had a hard time believing it was Jesse anyway because it did not seem like his typical character but he left us no alternative (remember we did not know he had AS at the time and that he probably was not sure what to do). We ended up spanking him for not admitting to it or giving the item back. We found out the truth after we sent them both to bed. As I listened outside their bedroom door I heard R.J. convincing Jesse that it was better for him to get blamed because he would not get in as much trouble as R.J. would. Needless to say, now R.J. had two things to pay for. The ability to recognize the value of deception does not occur until sometime in the early teens for a child with AS. Typical children usually gain this insight much earlier.

It frightens me to think of how Jesse's childhood could have been if it were not my parents, my sister, and me, his own mother, as his initial caregivers. Nobody loves your child as much as you do, except for Grandma and Grandpa! If Jesse would have been in a typical day care situation it could have been disastrous. One thing I can picture is that he would have likely had major sensory overload in a center with all kinds of noises, lights, smells, and changes happening without warning. Jesse did do one thing that I now know is typical of ASD, which was throw horrible tantrums complete with ear piercing screaming. *I* had a very hard time coping with that, I cannot even begin to think of how a daycare provider would have. I still feel guilty about how I dealt with his tantrums when he was two and three. I would put him in his room and hold his door so he could not get out until he finally calmed down, which would be only when he had been screaming and crying so hard he wore himself right out. Poor little guy, he had no other way of telling me what he needed or that something was just too much for him to handle. I was not able to hold him when he was acting like that because he would not allow me to. He had the vocabulary of a typical toddler, but he did not know how to express himself or ask for what he wanted. This is one situation where knowing he had AS would have been very helpful. I still would not have liked the tantrums or screaming but I probably would have known how to prevent a lot of it by knowing that he continuously needed routines and structure and not so much chaos at times. I could have also controlled more of the sensory concerns.

Fortunately we always have been a pretty structured family. I am definitely not a spontaneous person. Anyone that knows me could verify that! Bedtime has always been the same, dinner basically the same time, evening schedules very much routine etc. If we are planning a family camping trip I will have five lists written up three weeks early from what to eat, what to pack, what to do with the yard and house before we go, what activities we will do, even what to do the morning we are leaving. I do not go anywhere or do anything without a list and plenty of notice to everyone involved. This compulsiveness of mine has at least served Jesse well.

It is so important that teens, especially ones with AS, receive a lot of positive feedback on social competence from parents and peers. This builds independence and confidence. Most teens with AS need guidance and preparation for what to do and say in a social situation. Just as I sometimes try to guide him with friends, I remind Jesse often that he needs to let his employer know as soon as possible when he needs time off work. I also make sure Jesse knows how much his employer values him by telling him the good things they tell me about him working for them. I want him to feel confident that he is *doing it right* and to have the desire to continue to make an impression on his employer. Most parents are not going to know their child's employer personally like I do but you can still encourage your teen by telling them how responsible they are by getting to work on time, looking nice and working hard when you know that they are.

A child with ASD or any other disability can take immense amounts of time and attention in a family. It is so important to do everything we can as parents to have time for our other children and our spouse as well. Most often that is easier said than done for many families. Every one of our children needs and deserves their own special relationship with each of their parents. And every couple needs and deserves time together without the children. So how do we accomplish all of that when one child requires so much of our time? One suggestion would be to get outside help. You could possibly find a daily or weekly organization or group for your child to participate in for a few hours to give the other members of the family time to spend as they wish together. You may be able to find ideas in the local phone book or on the internet. The schools and church organizations in your area would likely have ideas also. If that is not an option you might be able to trade day care with a neighbor. Take their child during a time your child is at home also, if you can handle both. Then have the neighbor care for your child while you spend time with one of your other children, or your spouse. A lot of moms would probably love to have a couple of free hours a week and might be very willing to swap with you. Extended family is of course always a good resource also. Just be sure that whoever is going to care for your child knows and understands his challenges.

Having things at home as consistent, routine, and predictable as possible may also give you more free time since your child would know what to expect and would not be anxious as often. If they are comfortable and feel safe at home they can very often entertain themselves for extended periods of time. During that time you are free to have one-on-one time with another child or your spouse.

Family vacations can be another valid concern when you have a child with ASD. They can be an enormous source of anxiety for your child. A vacation means change in routine, unpredictability, unfamiliarity, and being around a lot of people and noise (never good). Our family has always enjoyed going on camping trips for our vacations which works out quite well. Jesse loves to camp and it is very quiet, peaceful, and relaxing since he only has to deal with his family. We keep things as routine as possible such as eating as close to the same time as we would at home; eating the same foods we would at home; keeping bedtime routines as much as possible; and even going to the same camping areas so they are familiar. Jesse can totally be himself and not have to go along with what a crowd is doing such as he would at a theme park or other tourist filled area. There also would not be as many sensory issues to deal with.

Did you hear the one about the little boy with autism who went camping for the first time? Standing outside his tent amid a beautiful pine forest, he wailed, "I hate it here! It smells like floor cleaner!"

Camping is not everyone's idea of a vacation. If your family would like to experience alternative vacationing choices there are some things you can do to make it more successful and enjoyable for everyone. Prepare your child with AS as much as possible. Tell him where, when, how long, what it will look like (show him on the internet or with brochures if possible), what he will be eating, where he will be sleeping, who will be there, what he will be doing, how you are getting there, and every other detail you possibly can. If you will be in a crowded and noisy area bring ear plugs for him and watch for his signs of stress to know if you have to leave that situation quickly. Try to keep a routine as much as possible on the trip or at least let him know ahead of time what he will be doing next. As they get older most teens with AS are able to handle a lot more than when they were young. You may choose to leave your child with a friend that they know well or a close relative during family vacations until they are more ready to handle it and enjoy it. Of course, you would still have to prepare your child for the time they would be left at "home" but it would most likely be a more familiar and comfortable situation for them regardless.

We are fortunate that we can treat Jesse pretty much the same as our other children. He is very capable of being left alone. He also adjusts to new situations very well now that he is older. He is even anxious to be on his own and live away from home when he goes to college soon. (His mother is not as anxious!) We are free to come and go as we would like with him or with one of the other family members, so that has not been an issue for us.

My issue as Jesse's mom is that I am always excessively concerned about him. I spend so much time and energy wondering how his day went that I cannot just relax. The difference in my concern for Jesse compared to my concern for my other two kids is that I know that they can and *will* tell me when something is wrong, or at least I can get it out of them. Jesse can't and therefore won't. I am sure most parents of a child with ASD can relate. These children just plain and simple do not have the same communication skills of a typical person because of their AS. I also know my other two kids will claim attention when they need it, and they will usually ask for help if necessary. The basic line is this: I can communicate with R.J. and Tonisha anytime that I or they need or want to. I do not have that luxury with Jesse. That is when a parent who has a child with ASD needs to take a step back, breath, pray and trust in a higher being to keep an eye out for their child since we just really have no way of knowing what is going on in their lives, or their thoughts, so much of the time. My faith is the thing that gives me serenity.

I was always satisfied that Jesse seemed content being by himself so much. But now I try to give him attention every opportunity I get because I do not know if he really is happy being alone, or if he is in fact quite often lonely. I do know that he needs his down time, especially after seven hours of conforming at school or a long day at work. His first two jobs have been perfect for him. At 15 he worked in the onion field's right by our house with a couple of his friends. He got to choose his own hours every day working as little or as much as he liked. He also had his friends all over the field so he was not *alone* but he was still basically by himself and did not have to worry about socializing. His current job, from age 16 to 19 so far is in a warehouse with a small crew of two secretaries and two other men who are a lot like him, quiet and easy going. His boss is very patient and understanding and they get along great. In fact, I was told that Jesse had job security for as long as he wanted it there—they love him! Jesse has some traits that unfortunately very few teenagers have anymore in the work force. He is a very hard worker, always on time, dependable, honest, kind, respectful and grateful. Jesse is very excited and appreciative of being able to earn money and he makes sure he does earn every penny of it. He realizes he owes his employer, not the other way around.

Jesse's differences have meaning and can teach us so much. He is a model of acceptance, open mindedness, humor, admiration, determination, and love. We have a saying in our house that is: "There is no such thing as normal." Who is to say what normal is anyway? By what standards do we go by? Who gets to choose? God only gives us what we can handle and I am very honored to know that He trusted me with Jesse, as well as my two other children.

There are many parents and other care givers who are strong, sacrificing, loving, patient, high-quality people who give these children their complete dedication. If you have a child with ASD or any other disorder and you feel guilty in any way, give yourself a break. Realize that you are the most significant person in that child's life! If you are reading this book you obviously care about your child and want to help him or her.

I know it is a gift to have Jesse in our family with his AS characteristics as well as his typical ones. He is so successful in his everyday life because he works so hard at it. The circumstances that people with AS are under are probably very strange. When they choose to deal with the world in the way that is expected from the human race they would have to be very intelligent to figure it all out. If you take the time to recognize how unique, loving, smart, fun, strong, and motivated your child is, you will know that having a child with AS could be the best thing that has ever happened in your family!

CHAPTER SIX

Causes

I, along with many others, do not believe that all children who have ASD are born with it. Many mothers have spoken of how their child was developing on schedule and was very alert and affectionate until they were given their MMR vaccinations. They immediately took a drastic transformation after receiving them. I cannot say if this would be the only, or even main culprit, or if vaccines are even responsible at all. But I do believe that *some* readers have probably experienced very frightening and confusing experiences after immunizing their child. Could it be coincidence? Could it be a factor? Could it really be nothing? I believe there may be more than one cause but vaccinations are still very much on the table. We simply do not have enough information or answers to what causes ASD at this point.

I do not believe that *my* son was simply born with AS. My personal belief is that it is the result of genetics coupled with an environmental factor such as toxins which our children can obtain from vaccines or other factors such as pesticides, foods, amalgam fillings, flame retardant materials, chemicals from cleaning products, and even the air that we breathe. We are subjected to numerous hazardous environmental exposures. It is possible that these toxins can also come in utero during pregnancy which would explain the babies that seem to have signs of an ASD immediately after birth.

Mercury, in small amounts, is everywhere in the environment. It is even in our soil, air and water. However, the biggest source of mercury exposure to our infants is in their vaccinations. Thimerosal, a preservative used in vaccines, contains approximately 50% ethyl mercury. In one day, some infants receive up to 100 times the EPA recommended safe level of oral exposure of mercury based on weight for an adult. Of course not all children who receive vaccinations are autistic, which would only show that most infants can handle that toxic load. It is those with the right genetic mix or predisposition who are adversely affected.

I am not advocating doing away with immunizations. We cannot let other illnesses become epidemics again. There just needs to be many changes in the way it is done. Infants should be tested to make sure they are free from infection and fungus. We need to make sure the child's glutathione (a natural antioxidant in the body) levels are high. If the child has low glutathione, which most kids with ASD have, we should not vaccinate. We need to realize that shots are not "one size fits all." There also needs to be safer vaccines introduced with **much less** mercury or aluminum.

I remember thinking it was a little odd the day Jesse received his 24 month vaccination. Right up until he had the injection he was very happy and playful, then right when he got the shot *everything* totally left. He was basically lifeless. He didn't scream, cry, laugh, talk, look to me for comfort, or anything at all! He seemed to get back to "normal" by the next day, but I will never know what kind of effect it may have had on him or if it truly is to blame for the onset of his AS. I know it does not make any sense that anything would happen that suddenly, but I know what I experienced.

I have a close friend who was terrified during both of her son's vaccination experiences, at separate times. In both cases they developed fevers (which is often to be expected), but more frightening than that…neither one of them would stop screaming for hours. On both occasions she went through the next 24 hours or so with them screaming like something was horribly wrong. Both times when she called the pediatrician she was told that was to be expected. Another friend had a similar experience: The day her son received his 24 month immunizations he developed a fever of 102 which lasted for three days. How can this not be doing any harm?

A mother knows when something is not right with her child. To quote the actress Jenny McCarthy, and many others: "When will people start listening to what **mothers** of children who have ASD have been saying for years, which is…We vaccinated our baby and SOMETHING happened. Something happened. Why won't anyone believe us?" I feel it is pretty obvious why nobody will believe us… If it is eventually determined that an entire generation of kids was essentially poisoned, a class action suit against the federal government could come about to the tune of hundreds of billions of dollars.

The evidence as it stands is already strong enough that regardless of whether a positive or negative association with ASD is ultimately proven, no form of mercury whatsoever belongs in vaccines given to children.

I was very thankful, and actually surprised, at the wonderful nurse at the health department who did not judge or guilt me for getting a release form to exclude my daughter from her junior high admittance vaccinations. The nurse was actually very sympathetic and understanding of the fears parents have with vaccines. I heard on the news of mothers who actually hold "chicken-pox parties" even now in the twenty first century to expose their children to the disease and get it over with, even though there is a vaccine for that now. Good for them. When I was young there was no such thing as the chicken pox vaccine and just about everyone would get the disease sooner or later. As far as I know, most everyone lived through it just fine. I even had to take my turn at ten years old during Christmas vacation, which was not pleasant, but I got a lot of attention from it! It was just part of life. I do not believe in putting unnecessary chemicals into our bodies. There are many diseases that are very notably life threatening, or life altering, especially for certain people and we do need to be grateful that we have vaccines to protect us from those. But I do not believe in being over vigilant and thinking we should expect to live through this life with no sickness at the peril of other risks from vaccines. Even the "completely safe" flu shots have mercury in them.

I do not believe we should never vaccinate. There needs to be some exceptions though and also much more research on making vaccines safer. I do not feel like *everyone* needs *every* shot that is available. My husband gets the flu pretty brutal a couple of times each year and has a hard time getting over it. I on the other hand have had the flu two or three times in my entire life. There is no justifiable reason for me to put that vaccine into my body and if my husband wants to try the shot or would rather live with the flu that is totally his choice. Of all the many times he has had it he has never gone to the hospital. My three children have never had the flu shot and not one of them have ever caught the flu, not even from their dad. My oldest child is twenty one; I think that is pretty good odds. I am sure there are some people who would be at great risk without the shot, but there are probably many more that would do absolutely fine without it. This is a personal decision; I would just hope that we would give it some thought before automatically putting *all* these vaccines into our children.

The vast rise in autism began in 1990…Why is that? In 1990 Haemophins influenza B was added to the vaccine schedule and in 1991 hepatitis B was added. Thimerosal exposure increased by 150%! Previously children received 11 vaccines in their first six months, now they were receiving 28! If there truly is a rise in ASD's, and many believe there is plenty of proof of that, it strongly implicates an environmental component to this disease. There is just no other explanation.

ASD can no longer be viewed as an entirely genetic illness with the outcomes written in the chromosomes. If we can find which factors are triggering the epidemic, then we can eventually prevent it and possibly even find a cure. The most likely scenario for the development of ASD involves a series of negative responses to the environment in a baby who is at risk genetically. As in most diseases, coupling genetic predisposition with environmental factors raises the risk. Look at heart disease for example. A family history of heart disease coupled with smoking, obesity, poor diet and low exercise makes ones risk substantially higher than genetics alone.

Research strongly shows a higher rate of autoimmune disease in the families of autistic children. I myself, Jesse's mother have an autoimmune disease and so does his grandmother. This may suggest a genetic predisposition in the immune system of a child with ASD. Some children's immune systems are simply not strong enough to handle the toxic overload of thimerosal. Children with ASD have abnormal detoxification systems, which also increases their risk of damage from environmental insults. There is some evidence that allergies to certain foods could contribute to ASD symptoms. Most people who believe this theory feel that gluten (a wheat product) and casein (a dairy product) are the most significant culprits.

There are studies showing that viral infections can also cause toxic metals to move to the brain. Other studies show that certain commonly undiagnosed bacterial infections in these children's intestines can make toxins like mercury even more toxic. If a child is born with an infection that no one can see and we vaccinate them while their immune system cannot sufficiently fight the toxins or viruses being injected, there certainly is not going to be a good outcome. It is the same concept as when you take your child to the doctor to get their shots and the doctor says he cannot immunize because the child is sick...Why is that doctor? He would tell you that the immune system is fighting something else and cannot handle the shot. So why would it be so hard to believe that some children are born with an infection or yeast overload, especially if there are autoimmune problems in the family history, and they cannot handle the first shot they are given right after birth? Or even for subsequent vaccinations, could there be an unseen infection that needs to be cleared up before immunizing? Is it too hard to believe that some kids are more vulnerable to toxic overloads than others are? Can't we assume that not *all* children can handle all thirty six shots? At least not on the time schedule that is largely required?

I have read where some of the medical field, and many scientists, believe that the digestive canal can even be linked to causing problems in the brain resulting in autism. Jesse had numerous issues with his gastrointestinal system as a child and I have learned that it is actually a very common problem in children with ASD. In *Bryan Jepson's book: Changing the Course of Autism, A Scientific Approach for Parents and Physicians,* he clearly states that there have been many studies showing evidence of children with ASD having high incidences of bowel pathology including abnormal stool consistency, diminished digestive enzyme activity, intestinal permeability, intestinal dysbiosis and painful inflammatory disease. He states that it is unclear whether the GI disease is a primary event or is secondary to an underlying immune system abnormality. It is known that there is a gut-brain connection such as established in other diseases (such as celiac) which would clearly signify that it is possible that the neurological effects of ASD are secondary to a widespread immune activation started in the gut. There could also be injury from neurotoxic compounds derived from food substances or abnormal bowel microflora. Most physicians who on a regular basis care for the medical needs of children with ASD do agree that treating the GI disease results in significant improvement in core autistic behaviors.

I cannot know with a surety if it could have been my son's immunizations that polluted his body, or if it may have been his GI problems or immunity issues, or even another environmental factor that contributed to his AS. But I very strongly believe that it was more than *just* genetics. I even question his dental work as a toddler. Jesse received a couple of fillings at a very young age. Mercury is continuously released from amalgam fillings and that alone makes them a health hazard. Mercury is the most poisonous, non-radioactive, naturally occurring substance on our planet. There is no safe level of mercury because even just one atom of it in your body is doing harm. Mercury can directly or indirectly cause, contribute to, or make worse every health issue we would ever deal with. Isn't it ironic that regulatory agencies require that the materials that make up amalgam filling, such as mercury, silver, zinc, copper and tin, must be placed in a hazardous waste container when it enters the dental office? Or that old amalgam filling pieces that are removed from a tooth must be placed in a hazardous container... but there are no regulations of an amalgam filling for when it is placed in a tooth! Doesn't it sound logical then that when an amalgam filling is placed in a tooth it basically turns that tooth into a hazardous waste container also? If I would have been a more attentive mother and understood this sooner I would have never had the dentist fill his baby teeth.

After watching home videos, I believe the contamination that led to Jesse's AS happened later than eighteen months, probably even twenty four. When I think back to his infancy and early childhood I cannot remember anything out of the ordinary until after the age of two. Even then, I had to really test my memory.

It is a common belief that ASD can have a late onset of symptoms so there is really no way of knowing *when* the child *really* got it...That is really interesting to me; I question if ASD's *truly* do have a late onset of symptoms, or if that is what advocates of "ASD from birth" believe, since it is common knowledge that some children do not show any signs of ASD until months or even years after birth. If a child *does* contract ASD from an environmental exposure (likely because of a genetic pre-disposition) and therefore *that* is truly the beginning of the disorder, of course the symptoms would not have been there previously because the disorder wasn't either.

If Immunizations had anything to do with Jesse's case, I delayed the onset of AS for him because I was not as proficient at getting him immunized as I should have been. All I know for sure is that Jesse was very interactive and right on schedule with every other toddler his age until sometime after 24 months. Looking back I can remember his tantrums beginning around that age, which is pretty typical anyway. But his did not end after the "terrible twos" and they were very intense. He also started having intestinal problems around 36 months. I have heard many stories from parents where their child showed a major decline or had a horrible episode very close to their eighteen month shots, or even twenty four month shots. Isn't

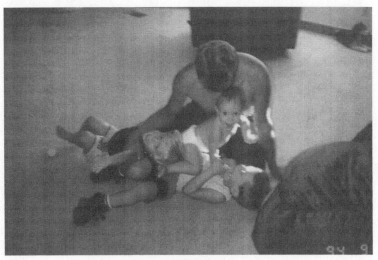

Jesse, Tonisha & RJ wrestling with Dad.

it possible that their bodies were not in the best health to deal with so many vaccines? Why would doctors have you sign a waiver every time you get vaccines for your children if they are so safe? Doctors, along with the government, need to stop deceiving parents by making us believe that immunizations are "free." *Every* medical intervention costs the body something. The American Academy of Pediatricians knows vaccines can have very dangerous side effects but they are too involved with the pharmaceutical industry to actually do anything about it.

Rubella is actually known to have caused cases of ASD. If rubella can cause ASD in some children and moms have claimed that they lost their child after the MMR vaccine (measles, mumps, rubella), which has three live viruses including rubella, how can we go on ignoring the fact that it is very possible that vaccines trigger ASD in some children? The medical community, along with the government, insists immunizations have no link to ASD. That declaration is not surprising at all. If it were in fact true that they did have a possible connection, this would be one of the biggest medical and political catastrophes in history. A government mandated program devastating the lives of thousands of children and their families affected with autism. The credibility of the vaccine program, many high-powered jobs, and large sums of money in potential lawsuits and lost revenues would be at stake.

Regardless of what we believe about vaccines or other environmental possibilities, many studies have established a genetic component in the development of ASD. There are many cases where more than one relative will have ASD or signs of one as close as the mother, father or other siblings. Studies of monozygotic (identical) twins have shown that ASD occurs in both twins in 64 percent of cases. Among dizygotic (fraternal) twins, it occurs in both at a rate of approximately 10

Jesse and Amanda at a High School Dance

percent. These findings suggest two possibilities: the involvement of more than one gene and the influence of other, yet unknown, environmental factors on the development of ASD. If ASD came from merely a genetic defect, 100 percent of identical twins where one had it would be expected to both have ASD. Researchers have discovered a number of genes that appear to be involved in ASD's. Some may make a child more susceptible to the disorder; others may affect the brain development or the way the brain cells communicate. Still others may determine the severity of the symptoms. Each genetic error may account for a small number of cases, but taken together the influence of genes may be substantial. Some genetic errors appear to be inherited where others occur spontaneously.

We need to accept that it is not *just* genetics that causes ASD's. This is an epidemic that has taken over on such a massive scale that it is unfathomable to think that it could be genetics causing this. It is not possible for genetics to be the cause of an epidemic. There could very possibly be genetic vulnerabilities mixed with environmental material that is triggering more ASD's.

I feel that many parents may be more comfortable with the belief that it is entirely genetics to blame because if that was the case we would not have to feel the burden of responsibility for our child's ASD. We cannot *choose* our genetic makeup or know what can come from it (until after the fact), but we certainly can choose what cleaning products to use, what foods to feed our children, and which vaccines to give them. We have to accept that we could not have known any more how to protect our child from an environmental assault than a genetic one. How can anyone be to blame when *no one* knows absolutely what is responsible for the disorder? The good news

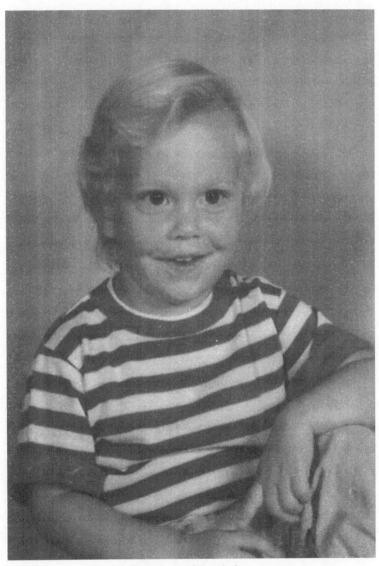

Jesse's 2nd birthday

is that most likely some day we will know, and that will be the day that parents *can* chose!

When did we become so trusting of the government and the pharmaceutical companies anyway? How many times have medications come on the market, been deemed safe, and then pulled off again due to major side effects? Sometimes even death. How could we possibly be so naive to believe that *all* thirty-six vaccinations given now are all completely safe with no dangerous side effects? The world has become so focused on "being green" and natural as much as possible, which is good, why not work more on that with our own health? Take the harmful garbage such as mercury and aluminum out of vaccines. We need to care for our own bodies as much as the planet.

There are many theories from environmental factors to genetics of what causes ASD but not a lot of scientific proof for any of them. There is even more controversy, accusations and blame, and flat out dishonesty. I have friends with completely different opinions than my own on the topic and it can be a very sensitive subject. I also have friends who feel the same as I do. There is just no way any of us can know for certain what the causes are until more research is done and the public is permitted to be informed of honest results. It seems likely, given the research so far, that several factors combine to cause ASD's. For example, it may be that certain children are genetically more susceptible to certain types of food allergies or more likely to react badly to certain environmental toxins. Until we have more definitive answers it seems to make sense to focus more on treatments and support researchers as they learn more. I would say with complete confidence that if autism (or Asperger's) is currently being claimed an epidemic, then that would prove that it cannot be entirely a genetic disease.

Jesse and Tonisha

There is just no such thing as a genetic epidemic. There is an environmental factor at work also, and finding out what it is (and it could very likely be more than one) could take decades. There is a great need for more research and there is still a lack of funding for it at this point. Although it is getting much better.

Until we have definite answers, I will always live with the guilt of wondering if I could have prevented my son from having AS by being more cautious and questioning about his vaccinations or by protecting him as much as possible from other environmental hazards whenever feasible. As a parent it is our mission to keep our children safe but it is nearly impossible to protect them from everything. I worry, like all parents of special children, that maybe there was something I did wrong or did not do right that could have prevented this. Did the doctor overdose him with antibiotics during his ear infections? Did the fillings in his teeth have too much mercury? Was there lead paint chipping from his bedroom wall that he put into his mouth? What about his diet, fluoride in the water, lactose intolerance, celiac disease, and on and on and on! We could drive ourselves crazy with the questions and what ifs. I do not know if we will ever know what caused Jesse's AS; but unless knowing can cure or alleviate his symptoms it does no good to speculate. I just pray that someday there will be more concrete information and even possibly a cure so that it *can* prevent a great deal more suffering.

Asperger's has become a very wide spread disease that needs much more consideration and research. It should have never been disregarded for so long. It is time to acknowledge the role of the environment in the rising rates of chronic diseases. As mothers and fathers of these children we need to take it easy on ourselves. Let go of the guilt. We had no way of knowing. We did not choose this for our child, and we certainly did not cause it either.

Jesse and RJ on family camping trip

CHAPTER SEVEN

We All Have an ASD

I knew that title would catch your attention. O.K., realistically, we probably would not all be officially diagnosed with an ASD, but I would bet every single one of us has more than one of the characteristics common to autism spectrum disorders! I would hope that we would understand and be more compassionate to people who suffer with these things on a daily basis, since we should all know how they feel in one way or another.

Who *never* has moments of confusion, embarrassment, or feelings of awkwardness in a social situation? How many of us do not like crowds or sometimes find it exhausting to keep up the "normalcy" and look right, act right, say the right things etc.? How many of us never lined up our pencils from tallest to shortest or put all of our Halloween candy in piles according to what it was? Who does not spend immense amounts of time on their passion whether it is fishing, scrapbooking, cooking, gardening or dinosaurs? Who has not had misunderstandings in a friendship or a romance? Can any of us say that we always understand what is being said to us and know just how to respond in every situation? Have you ever gotten so excited that you just burst in a way that might be a little overboard to the average spectator? I may not flap my hands when I get excited (as some people with AS do), but I have been known on more than one occasion to belt out the song *"I'm So Excited"*,

Jesse at Scout Camp. (seventeen years old)

by The Pointer Sisters; which I am sure those around me would much prefer me just flapping my hands! What about all our many OCD's (Obsessive Compulsive Disorders)? What about schedules and routine? This human race runs on schedules and routine, all of us. Who wouldn't be upset if they were happily playing Nintendo or watching their favorite television show and their mom suddenly ripped them from it to go get a haircut that they did not want or expect? Or, what about when your husband tells you he is taking you out to dinner so you get all ready and are anxious to go and he stops at a neighbors' house first to chat for 45 minutes... Our tantrum is just manifested in a little different of a way than kicking and screaming, hopefully.

What about food ordeals? I do not consider myself to be different or odd because I refuse to eat oatmeal mainly because of its texture and smell. And if I would happily pick a chicken sandwich for lunch every single day if it were available... so what! I can totally understand why my son refuses to eat mushrooms. I am sure there are plenty of other kids (and adults) who will not eat the slimy buggers either who are not considered to have ASD.

I had a very wise friend, who also has a son with AS, tell me how she dealt with the food issue. Her son would only eat a handful of things, which was not healthy or acceptable in her home. She believed he needed to learn how to adapt like everyone else in the family to what was being served. She was not unfair or ridiculous about it, after all everyone has legitimate likes and dislikes. Letting him just go without was not an option because he would shrivel away to nothing. She would give him the choice of trying the meal or having a cold shower. He would sit at the table until she would opt that he must be choosing the shower, but by the time she got

RJ and Jesse were inseparable when young

him to the bathroom he would change his mind and eat. This only took a few times before he willingly started to try many more foods and found that he was just fine with them. I have never been a short order cook and I firmly believe that when a mother goes to all the trouble to make a nutritious home cooked meal for her family they should *all* be expected to eat it. I am not so heartless as to intentionally make things they will not like, but I do not believe in pickiness at the dinner table either. Jesse despises pasta and my daughter Tonisha loves it. On the other hand, Tonisha does not like any kind of potatoes where Jesse would eat them for every meal. The solution is to have other things along with it that the other person likes and expect them to fill up on that, or have a little of the unwanted item along with it. No one is going to die from malnutrition if all they eat is rolls for dinner one night. My husband and I like both pasta and potatoes so it is very often that we are having one or the other to someone's demise. Our kids with ASD can adapt just like every child should be expected to. Sometimes it just takes a little longer and a lot more creativity to make that happen. One note of caution though, when a child (especially one with ASD) is about to gag on their food, they are not doing it just to provoke you or to get out of eating, they honestly can't stomach it!

When it comes to sensory issues…how many of us like it when someone suddenly screams close to our ear? Or if the neighbors have the car stereo outside blasting at the top of the dial? Who has never bought a new shirt only to find it is itchy or just very uncomfortable and then return it? Wouldn't just about all of us prefer a pair of sweats for comfort compared to a skirt or a suit? How many of us can handle the extremely loud jets flying over our house (especially when we are on the telephone!) or the smoke alarm going off incessantly? Who

Jesse and Tonisha playing together

enjoys uncomfortably hot or extremely cold weather? Get the picture?

We all have these issues, the only difference is that people with an actual ASD have to deal with all or most of them day in and day out and fortunately we don't. But along with their idiosyncrasies come many attributes.

How many of us can say that we *never* lie or that we *always* do what we say? People with AS are generally very honest, reliable and giving people. They cannot see any logical reason to not tell the truth, which unfortunately can sometimes get them into trouble. The same friend who has the son with eating issues told me how one day her daughter said, "I love you mommy", and her young son with AS said, "I don't love you. I love my dad, but not you." Could you even imagine how hurt she was? He did not say it in a vicious or heartless way, just matter of fact. She even questioned him about it and he just kept saying, "I like you but I don't love you. I love my dad." After a lot of painful deliberation she finally realized that he did not like the things she made him do (such as chores), and she told him that was her job to teach him how to do those things. He would not change his mind about "loving her" but when put into perspective, she knows how much she really does mean to him.

It is hard for people with AS to understand how their actions may affect someone else. They can often offend unintentionally. We all have times when we "put our foot in our mouth" or make a jerk out of ourselves. The difference is that typical people could probably prevent the offense from happening if they think before speaking while people with AS have no idea what response they will get from just being themselves. They are sometimes very blunt with remarks to others, but only because they are being honest and see no

Graduation Day with best friends, Chandler and Colton

reason not to be. Jesse is always making come backs to things we say. While it is almost impossible not to laugh sometimes, some of them are not very nice at all. He does not mean them to be out right hurtful he just thinks he is being funny, and truthful. For example, my daughter will say, "Jesse you have a big zit on your face," and Jesse will say, "Well you have a big nose on yours." The zit will go away, the nose won't! Tonisha has learned how to dish it right back though.

Often people with AS do not see why they should bother to respond to something that they think the person asking should already know, so they just don't, which might seem rude. Don't we all feel like not answering "a dumb question" sometimes? Typical people know the rules of society and know that it is not acceptable to not answer, whether it is perceived as dumb or not.

I really dislike labels. We do need something to call "it" so that we can research more information, get medical attention, and have an explanation for our differences; but we need to be careful. Everyone could be labeled with something. We need to see the *person,* not the label. We need to learn to let go of judgments. I feel like sometimes we are so anxious to have a reason why our child may be misbehaving or acting a little odd that we are too quick to throw a label on them that isn't even valid. There sure are *a lot* of children with ADHD! I am not saying it is not a real thing, I know it is. I am just wondering if in some cases the child could be hyperactive because of their diet. Could it be possible that they do not do well in school because they just don't *want* to sit still for seven hours a day, or they are bored, or maybe they do not have a good bedtime schedule? There could be *many* reasons for children to have a difficult time learning in a school setting. Many parents justifiably worry that having a label will render their child less of an individual in the eyes of others. Or that they will be

Tonisha, Jesse and Bob at Dinosaur museum. Jesse is 16

thought of as a person with a disability first and second—*if at all*—as the person they know and love. Jesse does have AS and knowing that helps us understand him better which makes his life a little easier. Even so, that is only a small part of who he is. He is first a son, a brother, a nephew, grandson, and friend to many people. He has a whole load of assets, problems, talents, thoughts, feelings and character...the same as every other person on this planet, just as his following list of definitions illustrate:

Jesse's Definitions: (at about age 8)

MISERY is: when your brother or sister is annoying you and you can't stand it.

LONELINESS is: when you are alone and there is no one to play with.

SATURDAYS are: when you play Lego's all day.

PUPPIES are: when dogs have children.

BEAUTY is: a wonderful picture

PUNISHMENT is: when you don't eat your dinner and you have to sit there for over an hour.

RECESSES are: when you get a small break from school and get to play soccer.

QUIET is: when everyone is gone and you're sitting on the couch.

FENCES are: when your dog roams around wherever he wants and you have to put one up.

FRUSTRATION is: when you need to do a report and can't think of what to say.

SIDEWALKS are: what you walk on when you're going to your friend's house.

TIRED is: when you've been working all day and you're ready for bed.

Jesse with his student body officer sweater, 8th grade

Teach your child to take pride in their individuality. Your child with ASD may have some peculiarities that society does not always see as standard, but so what! Don't we all? Most of us are just better at hiding them or knowing when it is not appropriate to illustrate them. Our children with AS are very intelligent and have a lot to offer the world and they should be given every opportunity to show that. As my friend Brandy always says about her young son with AS, "He will only be as handicapped as we allow him." How wise.

I do not personally believe that AS or autism can be completely cured. Would recovery mean that the differences in the structure or functioning of the brain have been eliminated? Or does it mean that the individual's functioning is no longer distinguishable from what is considered typical or normal? No one claims to have eliminated the neurobiological factors associated with Asperger's (or autism) although it has been shown that intensive early therapy and learning experiences might cause alterations in the neurological system. Since we do not know what factors underlie ASD we cannot assess changes in them. Many people with AS have become very successful at developing their own strategies to deal with common situations that are particularly difficult for them. Yet they still differ from most people in the way they have to deal with such basic functions as learning and socializing. Many will always have difficulty coping with certain types of social-affective interactions such as dating and lasting romantic relationships.

For those who have AS, it genuinely does not matter the cause or the reason that they have been dealt this challenge to live with, they can still make the most of it and have very full and happy lives. Most individual's with AS are extremely adaptable people. Jesse has created his own personal catalogue of strategies to help him deal with common situations that he has found difficult. This has helped him be able to manage his life quite well. Although I am sure many things are still confusing and hard for him on a daily basis, he has learned how to blend into the social order so well that basically no one even knows he has this trait. There are many stories where parents insist their child has been recovered from autism or AS. That is wonderful that their child has progressed so much that they live very typical lives, have had their diagnosis reversed, and appear to have no remaining signs of the disability. I just wonder if it could be *completely* gone. We really have no sure way of knowing if the person still struggles in some situations although they have taught themselves how to adapt, appear unnoticed and become successful.

It is especially hard to know what someone with AS is thinking because very often they are not going to know how to tell you. I really do not know if that can completely change or be cured because it is who they are. It is the way their brain operates. One central trait of AS is having difficulty communicating feelings and thoughts, can that really change? Does it even matter? If they are 'cured' enough to live in the real world and do the customary every day things we are all expected to do, than perhaps full recovery is not even necessary. Maybe they do not even want to be recovered. Many are very happy with who they are, as they should be! The real aspiration should be to help people with ASD learn how to live and adjust to the world they live in as much as possible so they can have every opportunity of a full life. It is some of the rest of us that may need to change in the way of understanding and accepting other people's differences. People with AS can continuously be learning and experiencing new things from childhood on to help them in their adult lives to becoming as independent as anyone. Autism Spectrum Disorder is just as it says a very wide spectrum disorder. Some may never become as independent as we would hope, but most will be able to have some amount of self-sufficiency if supported and taught. Others will lead very conventional, independent and successful lives. Just as they are for you, some days will be much better for your child than others. We are all different and the closed mind of an able body can be the greatest disability of all.

CHAPTER EIGHT

Social Challenges and Anxieties

We all have our share of hardships and challenges. Try to imagine what it is like for a person with AS who sees life through surreal lenses that distort and confuse and alter the most simplest of activities. As they often use intellect instead of intuition they can be in a constant state of alertness and anxiety which leads to mental as well as physical exhaustion. If we consider the inevitable difficulties people with AS have with regard to social reasoning, empathy, conversational skills, different learning styles and heightened sensory perception, it is no wonder that they would be more prone to considerable stress, anxiety and frustration.

When someone has AS they are much more comfortable when social interactions are brief and have a purpose. When the purpose of being somewhere is no longer relevant the person with AS needs to be able to immediately end their participation. They are not comfortable "hanging around". Others need not take offense to their abrupt departure or ending of a conversation because none is intended. Things that are ordinary to most of us such as shopping, dating, driving, keeping a job, and visiting with friends can be grueling tasks for someone with AS. There is no magic spell to cure your child's insecurities in social situations; it is a matter of thousands of little opportunities and encounters that can build self-confidence and understanding for them. Parents and others who care for someone with AS need to be aware for them as much as possible and clue them into the social nuances that are so difficult for them to perceive.

Indecision over things that most of us refer to as trivial results in an awful lot of inner stress for someone with AS. For example, if we say "We'll have to see what happens," or "I will decide later if we are going or not," we do not realize how much stress the uncertainty is causing the child. They need to know what is going to happen as soon as possible so that they can prepare for it. As one of the teens in the chapter *Accepting and Welcoming Asperger's* tells us, if something throws his schedule, or plans off, it messes up his whole day and he pretty much just has to wait for the next day to get back on track. I do not always achieve this, but I do try to let Jesse know as early as possible any part of our plans that will affect him. The more anxiety we can spare him the better.

One thing that bothers me deeply is when Jesse comes home from school or somewhere else with 'that look' he has when something troubling has happened. I have no way of knowing if someone made fun of him, if he did something to embarrass himself, or if someone picked on him. A lot of the time it is very possible that it should not have even upset him but he did not understand the situation. Sometimes he probably takes what peers say as an insult when they are just goofing around or maybe even not meaning anything by it at all. Other children know when someone is teasing with friendly or unfriendly intentions while the child with AS usually cannot distinguish the difference.

If Jesse is embarrassed for something he did, he often does not realize that it is typical of all of us to make that same kind of mistake. One Saturday afternoon Jesse told me he was going to go cash his work check then go and buy himself some new shoes. This was actually going to be his very first time going shopping alone (other than the small grocery store or fast food restaurants a few times). I was a little nervous just because I am his mom and he *does* have AS, which equals social concerns. Nonetheless, I figured he needed to start doing these things on his own more since he would not be living at home much longer. He left the house confident and happy. About fifteen minutes later he walked back in the door without the shoes and had 'that look' I was just talking about. His face was all red and he did not look like the happy boy who left a little earlier. I asked him what happened and where the shoes where and he reluctantly, with embarrassment, told me that he forgot to take his check. I wanted to laugh at how serious he was taking his mistake, but I didn't. I could see that he was totally humiliated and I said to him, "Oh that is annoying isn't it? I hate when I do that!" Then to make my point get through even more that what he did was totally 'normal' I added, "Your *Dad* always forgets things!" He did go again and was successful and pleased that time.

People with AS regularly feel that they need to be perfect and do not give themselves room for error. They can feel tremendously foolish or out of place if they *mess up* and they do not know how to handle embarrassment. The worst thing in the world for them is to be singled out and seen doing something not right.

A very sensitive issue for people with AS is that they sometimes perceive criticism or rejection where none is intended. They may have difficulty seeing the difference between a disagreement with their idea and a dislike of them personally. Most people with AS have a very hard time predicting what will happen next and they cannot determine the true intentions of others or their desires. When Jesse is with others he has become very skilled at appearing rather sure of himself and of being capable of maintaining his sense of composure, despite the fact that he is most likely worried that eventually someone will discover him as an *outsider*.

Jesse has many friends that keep an eye out for him and he is respected by adults because he is a considerate young man, but I worry nonetheless. I see the confused look in his eyes often, even at home. The person with ASD will frequently appear anxious since they do not know what they are supposed to do or where the next blunder will come from. I never want Jesse to wrongly presume that he is being made fun of or belittled, but that unfortunately comes with the territory of AS and not being able to read people. In his case I would think that most often his worries would be from his own misconception because I know how well he is generally accepted. On the contrary, if you feel that your child is at risk of being bullied, tricked into doing things they would not understand, or any other potentially dangerous situation, do everything you can to remedy the situation before it is too late.

For a person with AS, being alone is a very effective way of calming down and is even enjoyable, especially if engaged in their special interest. The child's bedroom is truly a refuge. When they are alone in their bedroom any signs of AS will disappear. It takes at least two people to create social interaction and if there is not anyone to talk to there cannot be any speech or language peculiarities. If they are alone there is also no one to judge if the activity they are doing is too intense or strange. There would be no sensory issues since the child can control what goes on in his own room. There would also be sameness and routine. The furniture would be in the same place they put it as well as their other possessions (not a good idea to clean your AS child's room without their permission and supervision.) And they could follow their own schedule. I would imagine that practically any person with AS is happiest when they can be alone as much as they prefer to be. Since people with AS are so routine oriented they will most likely have specific times of each day that they prefer their solitude. Whenever possible it would be a good idea for children with ASD to have a room of their own for these reasons, even while attending college.

Consuming themselves in their special interest is one of the greatest pleasures of life for someone with AS. I can tell when Jesse has had an especially hard day by how he plays the piano that evening. I know he plays it purely for enjoyment a lot of the time, but there is a noticeable difference when he is unwinding compared to just having fun. There is actually a very small percentage ranging from 5 to 10 percent of children and adults with AS who do not have a special interest.

It is extremely hard for our kids with AS to tell us what they need. They may be hungry, frustrated, frightened or confused and do not know how to express that. When Jesse was younger he would just suddenly explode saying, "I'm hungry!" This seems typical of any hungry child except that Jesse would be on the verge of passing out and exceedingly agitated before he would say it. I did not understand why he would wait so long and be on the verge of starvation to say something until I learned more about AS and the trouble it brings about with communication. He literally did not know how to ask for what he needed. As he has gotten older he has gotten much better but he is still reluctant sometimes.

A person with AS who seems to take major emergencies in stride may become upset over any surprise happening, even a minor one. We were having hamburgers for dinner one night when Jesse was about ten. We were all eating quietly when all of a sudden Jesse exploded! His bun was falling apart (as they often do) and he could not keep his burger together. It startled all of us since we were all having the same problem but the rest of us seemed to be dealing just fine with the trauma of unmanageable buns. People with AS can often seem unemotional, but when something matters to them (no matter how small) they can be very dramatic.

Too often people wait until something goes wrong before they do something about it. This is a completely backward approach for an individual with ASD. Prevention is the key. Anticipate problems, plan for them, and implement your plan before a problem arises. If you know your child will only eat McDonalds chicken nuggets and the family wants to go to a restaurant, obviously you will have to make a quick stop at McDonald's first if you want to avoid an uncomfortable scene at the restaurant when there are no McDonalds chicken nuggets on the menu. This would not be the time to teach your child to expand his tastes. That is a fairly safe example; much worse things can happen if our children are not prepared and taught what to do in different situations.

The child with AS who truly does not *get it* paddles against a brutal current in first comprehending and then executing. For example, they need to know that when someone at the junior high school makes fun of them or trips them (on purpose or not) they cannot punch them! I decided I better make sure Jesse knew what to do in case he got pulled over in his car by a policeman, so I asked him. His very witty answer was, "I wait until he comes up to the window then speed off!" He lets me know quite often that he is much more intelligent than I give him credit for. It is better to be safe than sorry. We are never quite sure what our teen knows or does not know.

An unfavorable AS behavior is usually a result of anxiety which can lead to difficulty moving on and letting go of an issue. This comes from the child's rigidities and is often the reason for behavioral problems. We have to replace rigidity with flexibility which is a skill that can be taught, and the earlier the better. Some reasons for rigidity in AS are as follows:

*Lack of knowledge about how something should be done. Not knowing how the world works in specific situations, the child may act inappropriately.
*The need to escape from a non-preferred activity or something difficult or undesirable. If they cannot be perfect at what they are expected to do, they will often refuse to try or participate at all.
*Violation of rules or rituals. Changing something from the way it is supposed to be. Jesse used to insist that we play games exactly according to the written rules, even when everyone participating was in agreement of how to change one. As he has gotten older he has become less rigid with that.
*Anxiety about an upcoming event, even if it seems trivial to most people.
*Misunderstanding or misinterpretation of someone's actions or words.

Attention getting is virtually never the motive for rigidity in AS. There is always another reason for the behavior. Consider all of the above explanations when trying to figure out your child's insistence.

When dealing with someone with AS who is angry it is imperative to know that some actions can cause feelings of anger to amplify; including raising your voice, confrontation, sarcasm, being emotional or using physical restraint. Nobody reacts well to these actions, but with someone who has AS it is almost guaranteed to 'add fuel to the fire'. I remember one bad episode I had with Jesse a few years ago where all of these things took place and I can say with surety that this statement is very true. What made it worse was that I did not even realize at the time that I was handling things completely wrong. He and I both ended up with very hurt feelings that could have been spared if I would have realized to keep calm and use logic (which works with AS) instead of emotions. Sometimes asking the person, "What is the matter?" can also inflame a situation. When experiencing difficult emotional distress the person's ability to articulate the cause of the anger can be significantly diminished and create further frustration.

Another area we need to prepare for is when other people do not know about our child's ASD. Understand and keep in mind that fitting into our social world *constantly* requires tremendous effort on your child's part. We cannot wait until our daughter gets into trouble at the high school for disregarding the principal before we let the school know about her social deficits. She will be very confused and frightened when she is being led into his office and receiving discipline and she has no idea why. I am a little bit of a hypocrite on this point because I have never disclosed Jesse's AS to any of the school staff. I reason that we need to use a little common sense and trust our own instincts and knowledge on who needs to know. It would probably be a good idea for at least one person in the school system to know in case there is a problem. I do not feel that it is necessarily a good thing for the entire staff to know, unless your child has some troubling issues. In our case, Jesse had never had any problems with students or the staff throughout school. We know that he has learned how to control his anger, so that is not an issue and we also believe he was always well adjusted and relatively secure at his schools. As their parent you can use your own judgment of who you feel needs to know about your child's ASD.

Most adults are very understanding and compassionate, but there are a few that may even subconsciously treat your child differently if they know about their ASD and do not understand it very well. I was actually very offended when a lady in my church who had always been my good friend said to me, "My son just told me that Jesse has Asperger's! Is that true?" And when I told her it was she said, "Oh that would explain it..." along with a giggle. Explain what exactly? She had known and thought highly of Jesse for nine years why should that be any different now? If she noticed something unusual about him why did it take her that long to say something to me? And what difference did it make now just because there was an actual title linked to him? He is still the same person he always was. It is really hard as the parent to not take these things so personally. We do not want to highlight the label or even acknowledge it at times. Our children are not a malady, they just happen to have one. No parent wants the stigma attached to their child that goes along with their condition, no matter what it may be. It was a very touchy moment for me and I was surprised at how disturbed I was, even though I know that was not her intention.

It is so important for people with AS to know what is expected, what to do, and how to do it to prevent them from 'losing it'. Along with that, anyone acquainted regularly with someone with AS must be able to determine when they begin to get anxious so that you can intervene before it escalates. With Jesse I try to make light of whatever it is that is *turning up the heat*. For example, if I tell him on Saturday morning that we are all going to work in the yard...right then...and I forgot to warn him ahead of time, I can be guaranteed to see a perturbed look on his face and know that he already had in his mind how that time was going to be spent. Accommodating abrupt changes in his day requires skills he may not have and can cause disruption from his whole routine. He would come and help anyway because he *has to*, but he would not be as enjoyable to be around and it would wreck his whole day by throwing off his plans. I can't always tell him ahead of time because sometimes I just don't know but I can help the situation by quickly adding that we are all going to go out and do as much as we can for just one hour (or whatever I can get away with) and then he will have the whole day to do what he wants. This always works because he then knows exactly what to expect.

I know all teenagers act this way when they do not want to do something, but the difference with most AS teens is that they are willing and want to please you if you are considerate of them. In fact, most children and teens with AS are very sensitive to being punished and in many cases have no understanding of what they even did to deserve it. Young children throw tantrums for a legitimate reason (in their eyes at least) because they cannot express what they need in any other way. Older kids with AS typically try to behave and follow rules and do what is expected of them. Not all kids with AS are the same, but characteristically most of them do try to be obedient. To be honest I cannot even think of any time we have had to punish Jesse since learning of his AS and understanding him better. We just have to know how to treat him and show him what is expected of him through *his* understanding of life, which is often different from our own.

We continuously need to explain how the world operates and why certain things are done. Then we have to convince our child why these ideas may be better than their own, which can be very challenging. Remember that your child with ASD acts the way they do because they have a different view of the world than we often do. They see things as black and white, no gray. They are also more concerned about objects and rules than feelings and ideas. If they have an opinion of the way something should be than you will have a very hard time convincing them any different. I have learned from experience that a child with AS will never get tired of arguing sooner than you do. Jesse does not do it in a malicious way, but he can come up with a rebuttal to anything we say when he is trying to show he is right about something. Most times we have to just tell him we refuse to argue about it anymore and he will luckily stop.

Many people with ASD have a real difficult time handling awkward situations such as being on a phone call where the subject does not interest them and not knowing how to respond or not knowing if it is acceptable to end the call or even how to do that. They may ask questions when they need to know something, but they are much less comfortable making "small talk" and in fact do not even see any reason for it. Human conversations and relationships can be very exhausting.

Many people with ASD internalize their problems, which often creates anxiety and depression. They tend to try to solve intellectual and social problems entirely on their own. Asking for guidance and help from someone else may not be considered as a solution. They become anxious when something happens and they do not know how to deal with it. People with ASD are rarely good reporters of the daily events that involve them. In any case, they are upset about something, do not know how to effectively deal with it, have difficulty asking for help (it doesn't even cross their mind that someone could help or would want to) and may even eventually act out in some way as a result.

We can always tell when something has happened to upset Jesse. What is very disturbing and frustrating to us is that we have no way of finding out what it was unless someone else knows and informs us. We cannot help him and we feel discouraged and useless. There is nothing worse than knowing your child is hurting and not being able to do anything about it. We can't just talk to him like most parents would because unless we ask the exact right question (which would be nearly impossible), he does not have the ability to tell us. I always have well intentioned people telling me to just talk to him and find out why he is upset. They just don't understand that it would be a one way conversation where, unless I already know what the issue is, there is no way to even start it.

Communication is probably the biggest challenge people with AS have. What I do try to do when Jesse is really upset is give him extra attention right away. If he comes home from school and goes right to his room without even looking for me first or getting a snack or anything then I know something is up. I do not want to give him time to dwell on what happened and get more depressed so I immediately invite him to run to the store with me or I tell him the dogs would love some attention (which makes him happy to receive their enthusiastic and unconditional love) or anything else I can come up with quickly. Generally, kids with ASD like to have some time alone when they have had an exhausting day of social conforming. In spite of that, I have found that the sooner I can cheer him up when he is really upset the better. The problem is that I cannot prevent him from thinking about it and dwelling on it later. I cannot minimize his pain and the hard things he has to endure every day through conversation like I try to do with R.J. and Tonisha. But I can show Jesse that he is valued and that we love having him around by spending time with him and showing concern for him.

Most people use self-talk and conversation with others to release their anxiety and worries. Many people with AS just do not have that ability and so they do not have that important outlet. They genuinely keep all their fears, worries, and upsets to themselves, which we can certainly appreciate how much that would add to their anxiety. It is really disheartening to me that Jesse is not able to communicate his feelings and just get it all out. The best we can do as parents is to build our children's self esteem the best we can so that they can deal with the downfalls effectively.

When your child with AS is really distressed the most effective emotional restoratives are solitude and becoming totally absorbed in their special interest. In a world that can be wildly unpredictable, the special interest is an oasis of predictability, calm and control. The special interest can provide a sense of peace, accomplishment, mastery, and happiness.

All people with AS are filled with anxiety, whether we see it or not. On the outside Jesse usually seems pretty happy to us, but I have to remember that things I take for granted are things he has to deal with every single day. Just communicating is very exhausting and complicated for him in general. Because of their neurological deficits, AS children and teens fail to understand their own feelings as well as those of others. The teen years are very confusing and stressful for all teens. The everyday issues more than double for the AS teen who has difficulties with social understanding and expression which significantly compromises their ability to converse. This lack of understanding, which results in frequent feelings of confusion as to how the world works, causes them to almost always be in a state of anxiety. Some of the ways that younger children with ASD may demonstrate their anxiety are by crying, hiding under furniture, clinging to you, bossing people around, hitting, throwing things, acting silly, or throwing tantrums. No matter how they display their anxiety you need to realize it is not an attention seeker or just misbehaving. There is always some distress, anxiety or obsession manifested in inappropriate behavior. They clearly cannot just tell us what is wrong.

As they get older, people with AS create their own structure and rules to help release their anxiety. Routines, rituals and rules give structure and predictability to what the person views as a chaotic world. The more they can control their own environment, the less anxiety they will feel. Nonetheless, there will always be uncomfortable aspects that cause distress. As parents we can do our best to recognize their sources of anxiety and get rid of them when possible. We can make the home environment as relaxing, consistent, and routine as possible. We can also prepare our child for different situations by letting them know what to expect and what to do. The more successful experiences they have the more confidence it will build and less anxiety will occur.

Routines are so important for our kids, all kids! But they are an absolute must for our children with ASD. Jesse has his place at the kitchen bar, like we each do, where he has eaten every meal since we moved to this home nine years ago. If I am sitting in *his* place doing bills or something when he is ready to eat, I can clearly see the look of uneasiness on his face and that he needs me to move. He is totally capable of handling the change when he has to but he doesn't appreciate it. He also always sits in the same spot to watch television. Even when I changed the furniture around he still chose that same location instead of the same piece of furniture. That kind of surprised me. Furniture can be a really hot topic with AS individuals because of their insistence on familiarity. I have a friend who bought new furniture for their family room and had to keep the old recliner just to keep her son with AS comfortable and secure. We have been very fortunate to have taught Jesse how to deal with new or re-arranged furniture from childhood because we did not know he had a problem with change. (So *that's* what all those tantrums were about!) I love to re-arrange the family room and we have also replaced our furniture a few times throughout the years. Now as a teenager Jesse will even change his own bedroom furniture around sometimes. He still refuses to have a new mattress even though his mattress is our old one and is now over 20 years old. It is important for people with AS to learn flexibility. After all, who can keep the same couch for sixty years?

Rituals keep someone with AS feeling assured also. Jesse's daily routine is exactly the same unless something untypical interrupts it. He can adjust for the disruptions, but without them his schedule would run like clockwork. Every weekday morning, while he was in school, he would go to the kitchen around 6:50 and watch the clock until exactly 6:55 then leave for the school bus. I had to set our clocks five minutes early one year because the bus kept coming early and Jesse refused to leave the house until 6:55.

People with AS generally have one or two great interests and that is what they spend their time doing. Their main interest is what gives them the most gratification and relaxation. We really need to respect their wishes with this, even when it means we have to listen to the piano for three straight hours every evening! I assume that my neighbors' eleven year old son with AS also has his own set of rituals. I see him outside soaring clear up in the sky on his huge swing set every couple of hours every day.

We want to give our children opportunities and new experiences as much as possible, but on a daily basis it is truly necessary for them to have their rituals and routines when it gives their life some peace and happiness.

CHAPTER NINE

Surviving Middle and High School!

As I mentioned in the previous chapter, you as your child's parent and advocate are the one who needs to decide who needs to know about your child's ASD when it comes to junior high and high school. Having an adult looking out for your teen might be very welcomed and useful or it might be unnecessary. This chapter is not going to focus on that topic since I have already mentioned it. This chapter is to help your teen make it through these very stressful and challenging years. This is generally the hardest time in any young person's life, but it can be potentially devastating and even incredibly damaging to a teen with AS. There are many things we need to know and that we can do to help them get through these years successfully.

The most important thing, for the children who realize and care, is that they have a friend. There are children on the spectrum who are so severely handicapped that they do not realize or care if they are alone; there are also those who *prefer* to be alone because they are much more comfortable and stress free that way. But the children who are desperately trying to fit in, be "normal", and accepted are very desirous of friendships. This is why it is very important for that group to develop coping skills, social skills and the ability to fit into some subgroup in middle and high school. If they are unable to do this their risk for depression increases. If your teen has not done this on their own, you may need to find them a group to participate in to learn these skills, or have them in counseling. A mentor, whether it be a peer or an adult, is necessary for survival in high school. A friend who can include your teen in their group will be saving them from the terrible years of loneliness in these critical adolescent years. There is nothing worse than being a sixteen year old (*who is aware*) walking the halls of the school completely alone every day. Having friends will also help save your teen from being singled out and bullied, which most often happens to kids who are alone.

Bullying has hit an all time high in this country and sadly the 'nerds' or the 'loners' most often have to deal with it entirely on their own because they often have no one as their ally. During a high school speech Bill Gates said, "Be nice to nerds, chances are you'll end up working for one". It is very unfortunate that while in middle and high school many kids do not see the logic in that statement or realize how vulnerable and insecure just about every teen really is, even the 'popular ones'. A lot of bullying happens at school, which desperately needs to change. The kids with AS often have a tendency to try to hide to escape the bullying by being alone, which is the worst thing they can do. They need to be taught to stay in, or at least near the crowd. Being alone makes kids so much more accessible and vulnerable to the bullying. Jesse has been extremely fortunate to be well liked throughout his school years and have many friends who watch out for him. Although I am sure some kids have thought some of what he does may be a little peculiar, he has always seemed to be very accepted and included. I would imagine one of the hardest things a teenager would ever have to go through would be to feel unwanted and criticized by their peers. There needs to be so much more acknowledgment and effort to stop the bullying as much as humanly possible in our schools. Whenever we as the parents are aware of such things going on we need to bring it to the attention of the school officials immediately and not use excuses such as 'kids will be kids' or 'it's just part of growing up'; including when it is our own child who is doing the bullying. We are certainly not helping our child by shielding them from discipline for such acts.

Do whatever it takes to make sure that your AS child has a friend if that is their desire. Even if this friend needs to be someone you seek out for your teen, it is absolutely imperative that they are not going this alone. Many adolescents are very caring and understanding and would be very willing to guide your teen through the middle and high school years. You can look for someone you trust in your church group or neighborhood or you can ask around if you do not personally know very many kids your teens same age.

In the church I belong to there are a few teens with different disabilities and I am always amazed and touched at how kind all the kids are to them. We had one girl, Michelle* who was crippled but was determined to do everything everyone else her age did. One year I was able to go to summer camp with Michelle and the other girls in our church as a leader and experience one of the most moving things I have ever seen. As part of the camp outline the girls were going on a seven mile hike in the mountains. This was not a flat, shady, easy trek either. We live in Utah, home of the Rocky Mountains. This group of teenage girls ranging from age twelve to eighteen went the pace that Michelle, using crutches, could keep up with which was extremely slower than any of them could have hiked. But what was truly amazing, every time they had to go up a steep incline a few girls at a time would take turns carrying Michelle. This was a very exhausting hike anyway, so going uphill was already a challenge. Imagine carrying a 110 pound person also. Every girl took her turn at helping Michelle get up the inclines, which were many, and never uttered a word of complaint. In fact, they all seemed honored to have their turn and had an attitude of sisterhood and love for each other. There have been many times in our church where I have seen these kinds of compassionate service.

If you and your teen are unable to find someone on your own maybe you could talk to the staff at the school your child will be attending and see who they could recommend. They know the students quite well and would most likely know who would be a good fit. Be as discreet as possible as to not humiliate your adolescent. They may very much desire to have friends but that doesn't mean they want someone *assigned* to the position. If they have been fortunate, your child already has friends and this most important factor is not going to be an issue.

Some children with AS will deny that they have any problem making friends (even when it's clear that they do not have any) or reading social situations. This is because they sometimes develop a form of over-compensation for feeling defective in social situations by denying that there are any problems. They may develop a sense of arrogance such as that the "fault" or problem is in someone else and that the child is above the rules that he or she finds too difficult to understand. The child really does know but will not publicly acknowledge that he or she has limited social competence. They are desperate to conceal any difficulties in order not to appear foolish. When these children are confused as to the intentions of others or what to do in a social situation, or when they have made a conspicuous error, the resulting negative emotion can lead to the misperception that the other person's actions were deliberately malicious.

Often out of fear of appearing stupid the child may have much difficulty admitting being wrong and may even be notorious for arguing. We have seen with Jesse that he will deny there are any problems. It is really important to him to appear as if his life is in total check. If he does get *proven* wrong he will appear a little embarrassed, usually grin a little, and then let it go. It is very commendable that he can do that so easily. If he is especially embarrassed or feeling put down, it won't be so simple. He will not argue or retaliate; he will most often head for the safest refuge and dwell on his embarrassment. As Jesse has gotten older he has gotten better at asking questions if he does not quite know what to do, or at least making sure he is right in what he is planning to do.

Basically all people with AS who appear to fit in are doing it by using their intellectual abilities rather than instinct to determine what to say or do. Their strategy could be to wait and join in after they have had a chance to observe carefully and know how to imitate what others were doing. If the rules change suddenly, the child is lost. Another strategy may be to avoid participation such as in a classroom by being very well behaved and polite so they are unnoticed and left alone. In school, children with AS have to work twice as hard as their peers, since they are learning both academic *and* social curriculum. Unlike the other students, they are using cognitive abilities rather than intuition to socialize and make friends. They can be increasingly aware of being socially naïve and making a social mistake. They worry constantly about social incompetence and conspicuous errors. This can lead to social phobia and withdrawal. People with AS are very often worried about what other people think, and that alone causes a huge amount of anxiety by always wondering what they did, or what they will do to make a fool out of themselves.

Your relationship with your child with AS through the teen years will be even more significant. It must be consistent in word and action so that he can see you as a predictable person, someone in control, someone who is calm and who keeps their word. He must see you as someone who is on his side and will help him understand the world around him. Someone who will protect him and always stick up for him.

Another important thing your teen must learn in middle and high school is how to maintain a low profile. They do not want to do anything to draw unnecessary attention to them self. This is most likely your child's biggest aspiration also. There is a very big difference in your child having enough self-confidence to be their own person compared to being *so* different that they are either in exile or severely teased and picked on. If we are being realistic and honest with ourselves we will admit that practically no one has the luxury of *total* non conformance. People with ASD generally already have a very difficult time fitting in and therefore should not add any unnecessary challenges. I am of course talking about the ones who are high enough on the scale to recognize that they are different and still have a desire to be included and accepted.

Your first job to help your child maintain a low profile is to make sure that he looks appropriate, which will help immensely. Throughout the elementary years it was likely that they could get away with pant zippers down and uncombed hair. While most children grow out of that stage before middle school, some children with ASD are not real concerned about those formalities clear into their teens. This is the time to *make sure* your child with AS has a good daily hygiene routine if they have not adopted one sooner. Jesse has a funny little ritual he does while brushing his teeth each day. He goes on a tour throughout the house while brushing. It's actually amusing since we never know when Jesse is going to appear with his toothbrush going. As long as it gets done, it's all good. If your teen has siblings close to his age then he already has an advocate to help him be "cool". If not, you must pay close attention to other teens in your area. You may even want to drop by the school on registration day just to get a glimpse of hair styles and clothing. The good news is, once your child establishes a daily schedule of hygiene practices, he will likely stick to it for life because of his insistence on routine.

Try to keep up on popular music, movies, video games and television shows at home so that your teen will be somewhat in the loop. We do not want to inhibit our teen's individuality or try to force them to conform; we just want to shield them from teasing as much as possible and help them to fit in and have friends, if that is what they desire.

School is the ideal place to provide direct social skills instruction for many reasons. It is the social setting that will be the center of most of your child's life, peers are readily available, and there are many daily opportunities for practice and generalization.

Many teens with AS learn how to "fit in" just by being around their peers and watching and replicating their actions. It is very important for them to blend in not just by looking appropriate but also by acting appropriate. Remember, children with AS do not have any physical signs of their disorder, which means their peers may not recognize that they have a reason for acting the way they do. The goal of most children with AS is to be accepted and seen as "normal", and the only way to accomplish that is by acting appropriate.

When Jesse became student body officer in eighth grade he and I went to get his group picture for the yearbook taken with all the other officers. One of the other boys came up to him and asked if they were supposed to put on their school sweaters or just have the picture taken in their student body t-shirt. Jesse just smiled at him and didn't say a word. The boy gave him a really confused look then walked off. This was one example of where Jesse didn't act appropriate. It is not only about not flapping their hands or speaking too loudly. Luckily, Jesse has learned since then that he does need to respond *every* time someone speaks to him. If he does not know what to say he will at least say, "I don't know"; even when it was not a question, but it still works usually.

The AS teen does not respond to or even notice peer pressure generally, which is great because they won't participate in illegal or immoral behaviors that they would not have any interest in on their own. They also do not have some of the self-esteem issues that many teens have from trying to fit in with the most popular trends. We just want to be vigilant in making sure they don't do unacceptable things that could promote teasing such as bringing an umbrella to high school or wearing the same shirt all week long.

Jesse is very conscience of fitting in. The last thing he wants is to bring attention to his self. He pays attention to what other kids are wearing and doing as well as hair styles. He chooses clothes that he knows his friends would wear. I can tell he is comfortable with that look himself as well, which is important. Jesse does like the typical teen activities but he has a different taste in music than a lot of teenagers. He likes classical music and classic rock, but he does know what is popular and being talked about because his brother and sister listen to that. Surprisingly he even has a friend or two with his same taste of music.

By the time our teens with AS have reached high school they really need to know how to let things go. We all know that life is full of disappointments, and by adulthood we have to be able to handle them maturely. People with AS have a tendency to dwell on things that do not seem right to them or are upsetting in any way. The teen years are an introduction to becoming an adult and there are so many times that we have to just "roll with the punches". "Let it roll off like water off a ducks back"; metaphors that someone with AS most likely would never get until you explain it. They have to learn to not be so rigid and that many things just do not matter; it will all work out. We can teach them through experiences where we are able to prove and explain that uncomfortable things happen, that we have no control over some things, and that they happen to everyone. They need to understand that it is not very often that they these things will be life altering or extremely serious. Teach them phrases such as:

Next time it will be better.
That wasn't so bad after all.
It is not the end of the world.
It could have been much worse.
Everyone deals with that sometimes.

Teach your child to observe their peers when they do not know how to act in a certain situation and use them for social cues. If everyone else stops clapping, he should stop. If everyone is starting to leave from a party then that shows it is time for you to go too, even if you wanted to stay longer. These sound like common sense things to most of us but to some people with AS they just do not come naturally.

Another common problem for people with AS is not being able to focus on one person's voice when several people are talking. In *Tony Atwood's book: The Complete Guide to*

Asperger's Syndrome, he tells of an instance where a child with AS was in an open-plan classroom that had two classes. The child could hear his teacher reading out a math test while he also heard the other teacher giving a spelling test. When his teacher got his paper she found that he had written answers to both tests. If your daughter with AS is sitting at the back of the classroom it may be nearly impossible for her to hear and to focus on *only* what the teacher is saying. She is hearing people around her, perhaps the lights buzzing, noises from outside and so forth. This can be distracting for any child but it is already a challenge for kids with AS to process someone's speech and meaning regardless. If you can make sure their teachers put them at the front of the room where the child can focus on them it will make a world of difference. They are much more likely to understand if they can concentrate on one voice. Even better is if they can have written instructions, but that just isn't always possible.

High school is when it is time to get down to business. You need to start helping your teen make plans for his future and helping him to be prepared for that future. By now you should know a lot better what is realistic and what is not for your particular child. Many individuals with AS have better than average IQ's, go to college, develop successful careers, and form lasting relationships. Others may continue to live with their parents or other family members, be unemployed or underemployed, and have very few outside acquaintances. Either way, things will change when high school ends.

Everyone needs a purpose. If your adolescent is not advanced enough to work in the community at a typical job there are places that hire individuals with very limited abilities. Many fast food chains, second hand stores, grocery stores and charitable associations have positions available. Employers are not permitted to discriminate; if there is a job your young adult could carry out, many businesses will give them the opportunity to try.

Many times your child's special interest, often bordering on obsession, is their area of strength and can get them very far in life. It is so promising if your child's special interest is something that can lead them to a career. If your teen with AS has a special gift or talent (which most do), high school would be the optimal time to start figuring out where they may be able to channel their skill into a career or livelihood. There are even possibly classes at the high school that would help them along further. If you can find a practical way to apply your child's special interests to the "real world", then his incredible abilities to focus, memorize and spend long hours immersed in that topic become invaluable strengths. For careers that rely on detail orientation, such as library administration, engineering, or computer science, having AS or high functioning autism might be a real asset.

Despite being notorious for becoming irritable over relatively trivial matters, some adults with AS are renowned for remaining calm in a crisis when many typical adults would panic. Think of how helpful that quality would be in a career of Emergency Medical Technician or working in an Emergency Room. This would be a great quality for a soldier on active duty. Help guide your teen in a direction of schooling that you can see they would be successful at and enjoy.

Jesse is making his own road map to his future and nothing has slowed him down. He knows what colleges he plans to attend and that he will settle for no less than his P.H.D. in Paleontology. I would have thought that Jesse would have chosen a career in music with his exceptional talent as a pianist and his love for it, but that is not what he chose. Ever since he was old enough to talk he has been referring to paleontology as his main passion. He would even call it that at a young age before we even knew what the word meant. It took me a little while to figure out it is all about dinosaurs. Many children with ASD have a love for dinosaurs for some reason, but his love was lasting. I would take the kids to the library to check out books all summer and Jesse always went straight for the adult section and came home with books on paleontology way above a normal seven year olds reading level. Jesse made his future plans without any help from us. It turned out to be wonderful that he had that much forethought and ambition on his own. I had been concerned that he would not be interested in going to college after high school, when all along he already knew exactly where he plans on going. He chose a college in eastern Utah that is talked about in his paleontology books and that will take him right where he wants to be for his future.

With the needed interest, support, and guidance, any career is possible whether it be a soccer coach, an astronaut, or anything in between. Your child thinks, views the world, processes information, and has a personality style that is different...but not inferior. Help your child harness their strengths to overcome the hurdles that stand in the way.

If you tell yourself something long enough you start to believe it. I have always told myself that Jesse would do everything that everyone else his age does, even when others have said he wouldn't. And he has. Now comes the real test for me, not him; preparing him to live away from home on his own and telling *myself* that he can! *He* already knows he can.

Universities are filled with people with AS. Where else but in college can you obsess about your interests and get rewarded for it? In what other setting can you create your own sense of style without looking like you missed the point? Where else can you talk to everyone you see, no one at all or even to yourself without missing a beat? In other words, where else can you be totally you and fit in like everyone else?

Begin teaching your child as early as possible the things they will need to know to live on their own, go to college and be independent. They will need to be able to handle spending significant time away from home; know how to handle finances; have a basic knowledge of cooking and safety; be flexible with food he will be served by others; know how to get around whether by car or public transportation; have a basic knowledge of house cleaning; and be able to handle problems that may arise or know how to find help. Many of these things should have been applied much sooner than high school such as house cleaning, simple cooking, and finances for example. Our children need to know how to deal with disappointment and change. Most of these things are things you can teach your child at home.

Jesse has learned so much through participating in Boy Scout s since he was eight. The camps especially were invaluable to him. He had leaders and was supervised, but he was still away from home, his parents, and his regular set routines. He had to be responsible for himself for days at a time. He learned how to pack what he would need, how to eat what was available whether he liked it or not, how to manage his spending money while there and make sensible purchases, administer first aid, how to keep clean and organized (relatively), how to ask for help or directions, how to cook, and many other valuable lessons they teach through the scouting program.

Jesse learned how to handle finances through first having jobs at home and later having outside employment and certain bills he had to pay. Since my children were old enough to count we have had them work at home doing household chores where they would earn certain amounts of money per chore. They were then responsible for purchasing their own clothes, entertainment, and pretty much anything they wanted or needed other than basic necessities of life such as food and shelter. It did not hurt them one bit. Seeing the proud expression on a ten year olds face when they hand the store clerk their own earned money for a pile of new school clothes is priceless! They learn very early that the $25.00 pair of jeans is just as good as the $80.00 pair when it is their own money. They take a lot more pride and care in the things they own because they had to work for it. It is no different than parents who give their children an allowance for doing household chores. We just took it a step further and taught them how to be frugal so that they could have what they wanted as well as what they needed. It was not all just to spend. Isn't that how life works?

Jesse has learned to be an extremely thrifty shopper and knows how to save for a rainy day. It is funny how your kids want to go get a hamburger for dinner until you suggest everyone pay for their own. We don't do this to be selfish, of course we buy them a hamburger once in a while...We just want to teach them that our money is hard earned also and we all can appreciate what we have and not be greedy or ungrateful. As a teen, Jesse has had to make set payments for his car insurance and a couple of other things which helped him get into the routine of budgeting and always being prepared to pay his set bills. It is so important to teach our kids how to budget before they leave home and to teach them the hidden evils of credit cards and borrowing. Jesse has actually learned the value of being able to be the lender instead of the borrower. He has benefited many times from R.J. or Tonisha needing to borrow money from him.

I believe our civilization would be very well served if every high school required classes on basic budgeting and financial sense in order to graduate. Unfortunately, sometimes children need to hear something from someone other than a parent to really listen.

It is also a very good idea to give your teen with AS a few pre-trial weekends while still at home where they are on their own if they are planning on going away to college etc. Here they are in familiar territory which is much safer to practice, but they are still responsible to take care of everything such as cooking, locking up the house, getting things in the mail, driving where they need to be, dealing with phone calls etc. If anything does go wrong there will be someone close by who they already know that they can turn to for help. You can also have someone check in on them if needed. We have left Jesse home alone often and he does just fine, but I am still very nervous about him being so far from home when he leaves for college soon. Everything will be so much different in a whole new town without anyone he knows and a whole new schedule and routine. I want to do everything possible to prepare him so I can limit his uncertainties as much as possible. Aren't cell phones wonderful!

CHAPTER TEN

Should You Tell Your Child They Have Asperger's?

This is a very hard chapter for me to write because I have teetered from one decision to the other for many years when it comes to telling. My husband and I just recently decided that it is absolutely necessary to tell your child; and the sooner the better. If you know of his diagnosis at the age of three it is so much better because you may just let your child grow up always knowing. If you are in the same position as we were and do not find out until they are in their teenage years, it is a much harder judgment call. Being thirteen and starting middle school, having major puberty changes going on, and needing so desperately to fit in with your peers is not the time to have confirmed that you are different and learn that there is very little you can do to change that.

Sooner or later every person with AS begins to notice that they are different from their peers. Typically it occurs in early adolescence. They are often happiest when alone because they can be themselves effortlessly. They have realized that they are *missing something* but just can't figure it out. It can easily cause them to feel detached from the world and isolated. Experts agree that adolescence is probably not the optimal time to tell a child they have a lifelong disability. Even though by that point most of them will have realized something is wrong, to be told you are different at a time of life when it is so important to be the same can be a devastating blow. On the other hand, parents who do not find the diagnosis until their child is a teen may not have any other choice. If your child is planning on pursuing a career or college after high school, knowing that they have AS could make things a lot better for them. There could also be different support as well as accommodations and training available if employers and colleges know. If you do choose to tell your child, it should be their choice of who else they want to know. Often it will create understanding and empathy; other situations may cause avoidance or harm. Usually by the time a child is in their teens their peers are mature enough to understand differences such as these better and have the decency to treat them with respect. Elementary children can also be very thoughtful and considerate. One teacher told a heartwarming story of a class of elementary school children who reprimanded a substitute teacher for not understanding one of their classmates with AS and treating that child too harshly.

We have struggled with whether or not to tell Jesse for the past six years and only very recently realized time was running out. He will be leaving home in less than a year and no longer receiving our daily self-confidence boosts or having us to protect him and explain things to him day in and day out. I am sure he has known for a long time that he is *different*, but I am sure he has no explanation as to why. It is so hard to know if it will help them to have a reason or if it will devastate them knowing what it is. I cannot even imagine what Jesse must have been thinking all this time when he just knows he has a much more difficult time fitting in where everyone else seems so naturally comfortable. Bob and I always felt that he was doing so well without knowing that we did not dare mess that up. We were terrified of crushing him or possibly taking away his capability of making his life work so well. Jesse has always been such a sweet, happy, giving person and we did not want to damage his spirit by telling him he is not like everyone else. In our eyes he has always been better! When I realized we could not keep it from him forever, since he really did need to know who he is, I came up with a plan that worked wonderfully!

I got on the internet and read what other teens had said about finding out, and I was pleasantly surprised. There were some negative results, but also very many wonderful ones. One teenage boy said, "Asperger's was a recent diagnosis for me and a great gift. It explains a WHOLE LOT!" Another boy said, "It's a great gift and you shouldn't hold back of who you are." A teenage girl said, "I was very upset at first, but now my life makes a lot more sense than it did before." My favorite response, which is from a 16 year old boy was, "I actually became proud to have Asperger's after finding out and reading more about it and I always felt smarter than everyone, or that I thought in a different way. Sometimes I feel sorry for people who don't have it because they might never see the world like I do."

The big decision comes when you ask yourself if you feel it is possible to tell your child without losing their independence and without permanent damage to their self-esteem. It is so important to tell them in a very positive way. Our personalities are all heavily influenced by our experiences, and unless we learn to cope with who we are by ourselves, there is a chance we may never gain total independence. We can't stop at being positive when telling them; we have to teach our child to be proud of their condition. Focus more on the qualities than the difficulties. Without doubt they already know a lot of the difficulties anyway.

The way we handled the "big day" was by carefully planning for it and having our other kids involved also. Our family has a family night once a week where we do different things and this time I had planned it in a way to "reveal the secret". Clear up until the last minute Bob and I still had doubts and fears, but we also knew that it had to be done and we were as prepared as we could ever be. I started by handing each person their favorite candy (which I knew would start things off right for Jesse anyway!) Next I explained how even though we all like candy we all have our different preferences. I told them that our different tastes, ideas, thoughts and personalities are what makes us who we are and unique. I had also set out a bunch of record covers (yes, I *still* have vinyl music records...) and had my kids say what was the same about all the groups. They said things such as that they were all men, all "old", all musicians, all have hair, etc. Then I told them that even though those singers all had so much in common they were still all very different from each other and even though they were all very famous there were still many things about each one of them individually that probably hardly anybody knew about them.

Next I pointed out how our own family, like every family, has things a lot of people don't know and that we may not even realize about each other or even ourselves sometimes. I talked about how one of us has OCD, another has ADHD and another has Asperger's. I don't think Jesse had even ever heard the word before, but it didn't matter. We talked about the strengths and some of the weaknesses of each person's "title" and saved Jesse's for last on purpose. By the time I was done explaining his he was grinning from ear to ear! I think Tonisha may have even been a little envious since I made it sound so great. I started by telling him a list of famous people who were all thought to have had Asperger's. I used his love and respect of classical musicians as the hook by telling him that Mozart and Beethoven, as well as other musicians with such great brilliance, were said to have had it. He was already caught but it got even better when he found out that Albert Einstein, Isaac Newton, Benjamin Franklin, George Washington, and Leonardo Da Vinci, where a few more added to the list. There were many others which also surprised him. He was quite proud to be in such good company.

I explained to him that some of his amazing qualities could come from his Asperger's. I also wanted to make sure he knew that many of his traits are just him regardless. I told him that we started wondering because he was always just such a smart and obedient kid! We told him that it is unique that he is able to memorize *anything*, and that he is so honest and respectful. I told him we have never had to worry about him lying to us or getting into any trouble, which is not always true for kids without Asperger's.

I paid particular attention to his feelings and behavior for the next couple of weeks to make sure we did not make a huge mistake, even though the initial outcome was so good. He did not seem any different one way or the other. I feel it was a good thing to get it out in the open but I am supposing he doesn't really understand what it all means anyway. How could he, I have been studying the subject for over six years and still learn more about it daily. I think little by little he might become more curious and want to search it out on his own. I would definitely expect that it *has* answered some of his questions. I do not know if he is disturbed by the diagnosis at all or if it is just another matter he simply heard about…I really do not know if it helped much, but I am pretty sure it did not hurt. I can count on him not asking us anything about it because that is not what he does.

I cannot tell anyone how or when to tell their own child or even if they should. But I do believe that it can only help them in the long run. I cannot even imagine how confusing and sad it would be to go through your whole life wondering why you are different from everyone else. Our differences should be revered, but unfortunately in the world we live in, they are often not. People with ASD need to know that they are not the only one with those problems to deal with. There are so many other people with ASD and if our kids need someone to talk to who thinks more like they do, those individuals are out there! You can help them find groups on the internet or hopefully even in your community.

Just make sure that your child knows that they should be proud of who they are *and* proud of having AS. She or he has many unique and amazing qualities that most typical people can only envy. It is a great gift and your child has potential for creativity far beyond the average person.

CHAPTER ELEVEN

Other People's Opinions (O.P.O's)

The child with AS may point out your mistakes, no matter who you are, and think that you should be grateful to them for doing so. They do not know better (until we teach them), but *we* do.

Everyone has an opinion about just about everything whether it be what Chinese restaurant is the best, which movie should have never hit the big screen, where the best place to ski is, and even bigger, more significant subjects such as politics or medical care (these days is there a difference?). But when it comes to someone expressing their opinion about something as personal as your own child or your family, sometimes it is hard to not take it too personally. Genuinely, most humans are very caring and would never say anything to hurt someone intentionally. But more often than not, when someone feels they are an authority on a matter they are actually quite often fairly ignorant about it...unless they have "walked in those shoes" or deeply studied the topic.

We all like to feel like we are helping and giving good advice, it is human nature. Naturally, many of your friends and relatives, even strangers, will offer you advice on how to raise or deal with your disabled child. My best advice (or *opinion* you could say) would be: Learn when to listen and appreciate it; learn when to smile and turn the other cheek; and learn when to slap them! Just kidding on the last one... Have a thick skin and realize that some people really do not have a clue what they are talking about, even when their intentions are good. For instance, when your father in law insists that the only thing your child needs to "straighten him out" is a good spanking, your father in law needs a lot more education on ASD. Even then he might choose to not believe it. It can be very painful to feel judged or criticized in the way you deal with your child, but you just have to believe that you are doing the best you can and most likely the best thing for your own child. You know more about him and his condition than anyone else does. How many of your neighbors have read all 30 books from your local library on AS like you probably have?

I actually had a psychiatrist tell me recently, very authoritatively, that since I have never had Jesse officially diagnosed by a *real doctor* (meaning a psychiatrist), that there is no way I could know what he has and that it was not AS at all but Pervasive Developmental Disorder-not otherwise specified; as if that would change things a great deal. I was offended at his implication of my foolishness for assuming that I knew the technical term for what my son has without having a "real" doctor tell me. I was also surprised at how assertive and certain he was in giving a diagnosis of his own after only meeting Jesse for a matter of minutes. This doctor knew relatively nothing about my son yet he was trying to force me to accept his opinion based only on his degree. This was one of those times I chose to smile and turn the other cheek.

Pervasive Development Disorder-not otherwise specified (PDD-NOS) and Asperger's are, when all is said and done, two different terms for relatively the same condition. In fact, PDD is often the heading for *all* of the ASD's, which would of course include Asperger's. Professionals seem to choose to call the individuals disorder PDD when they do not have a definite idea of which ASD it is. That would explain the added footing of "not otherwise specified". In *my opinion*, I would say that it is just a catch all term.

With all of the research I have done on ASD and knowing my son personally, I would say I am relatively qualified to make a decision of which disorder on the spectrum he fits most. It is not a matter of simple blood tests, unfortunately. When choosing a therapist or doctor to work with your child it is very important to find one that values *your* competency and knowledge about your child's condition and will appreciate your own insights from experience. You need to feel as if you are working together, not being disregarded or belittled in any way.

It is perfectly acceptable and even expected to feel angry, cheated, sad, discouraged, confused, desperate, and any other feeling you may have when you are dealing with your own child's disorder. Surely you will have days when those are the dominating feelings and other days you will have feelings of gratitude, love, amazement and enjoyment. Anger and discouragement are absolutely normal feelings when dealing with life's challenges. However, we need to recognize the joys and blessings that come from those challenges. I used to feel sorry for people with a special needs child until I got to experience myself what a blessing they are. These children are a gift we would have never thought to ask for. We learn and receive so much more from them then we could ever give back. People who have a child with a handicap are neither martyrs nor saints. A martyr is someone who makes a great sacrifice for a cause; no one when expecting a baby says, "It does not matter if it's a boy or a girl, as long as it has a disability." A saint is a holy or Godly person according to Webster's Dictionary… and I personally have not met anyone who is equal to God, even though most of us aspire to be. We are all just parents trying to raise our children like everyone else.

I used to be guilty of looking at parents of disabled children and thinking they must be extremely amazing people to handle that, until I finally realized that they did not have a choice. They were basic every day people just like everyone else who had received this challenge and they handle it because they have to, because they love their child deeper than anyone could love anything. I am not saying that many of these parents have not developed incredible patience, will, devotion and selflessness, because they probably have! I just believe that just about anyone in these shoes would do everything they could to make their child's life as fulfilling and happy as possible. I believe we are not given anything we cannot handle and I feel that parents who are required to raise a disabled or other particularly challenging child are blessed with the patience, strength, love, and determination they need to make it possible for them to do it.

There are frequently times that parents with a special needs child would very much welcome some input and opinions of what to do to make their child's or their own lives' less complicated. Unfortunately, those who we are close to and would listen to often do not deal directly with disabilities and will not have many new ideas. What is a huge help is to just have someone to talk to, unload on, and support you with babysitting relief or other ways you may need help. The places to go for helpful ideas and suggestions are where other parents facing the same struggles are such as the internet, community groups, books on the subject, and specialists in the field of ASD's.

Sometimes people believe they are helping you feel better and are honestly trying to give you comfort by "helping you see your blessings". They tell you how there is always someone who has it much worse or that things could even be much worse for you so you should really be grateful that they aren't. As true as this is, when you are having a particularly hard day, sometimes it just does not matter that it could be worse because right then it is bad enough. Ironically, it is not that Jesse has AS that made me feel this way or realize this truth. I have never felt extreme distress for the challenges AS brings because in our family it has brought more blessings than adversity. I know we have some bigger hurdles coming, but I also know we are very fortunate and I would not want to trade places with anyone.

I have felt these feelings through dealing with a perplexing medical issue of my husbands' for some time and I can certainly sympathize with people who have a child with many needs or difficulties. You do not want to hear all the time that you should "Be grateful it isn't worse", or that "Someone else has it much more difficult." Everyone has times in their life that they would much rather skip over. While you are suffering is not the time you want to also feel like you are complaining or that you have to put on a happy face at all times. Sometimes that is just too much.

Parents raising a disabled child do not have the luxury of the challenge finally coming to an end or having some chance of relief. This is their life. In their eyes it honestly does not matter that someone else has it worse because, at the risk of sounding callous, they are not that person. They are who they are, and they are dealing with what they have to deal with. It is hard, and frustrating, and sad, and lonely, and sometimes they just want some compassion and to not have to put up a front of being strong and thankful. There is a vast difference between being grateful and being unhappy. Of course most parents are very grateful that they even have their child and for so many other things in their lives. But that does not mean they are happy when they go for days on end without sleep or spend immense amounts of money and time trying to find the right doctors or therapy, or worry endlessly about their child's future, or when they have to see their child sad and suffering and there is not much they can do about it.

Acceptance of unpleasant truths is not something that comes easily to anyone. But achieving some degree of acceptance is vital to your long term prospects for happiness. Someone may have it worse, but we all have challenges that test us to *our* very limits; otherwise life *wouldn't* be fair. Someday we will understand the reason for the particular challenges we endure.

Our children with AS should be afforded a great deal of freedom and respect as they choose who and what they will become, without having to face opinions and judgments. There is nothing inherently wrong or undesirable about the need to live alone. There is no reason someone has to have countless friends to feel valuable. And there is not one reason why the term "normal" should not be an exceptionally relative idiom. Normal is often measured in terms of perfect and absolute standards, most of which are impossible for *anyone* to reach.

Often, people who have AS and are 'high functioning' are not even recognized as being different. However, we do need to recognize and understand the difficulties that they face because of their unique ways of thinking, doing things, and experiencing the world. Jesse is very high-functioning, and while I appreciate that most people treat him totally normal, I still want them to understand that sometimes he needs a little extra direction and help to know what is expected of him. I do not want him to have any more anxiety than he already does and if he is expected to just know things intuitively like most of us do, sometimes that can cause him a lot of stress. People with

AS do not have intuition, they have logic and re-call of past experiences. The more experiences that they are able to add to their library of memories, the more they can endure when that same experience comes again because they will have re-call of how to behave in that situation.

Many times when a child with ASD misbehaves in public it is reflected back on the mother. Strangers are wondering why that mother would allow her eight-year-old to act that way or why she does not teach him how to behave in public. Maybe they are thinking the child is just spoiled and needs a good spanking. After all, children with ASD look very normal, often even very attractive and have no physical signs of a disability. Of course we would never even think of judging a mother struggling with her clearly physically handicapped child in public. We would most likely have compassion for both of them. This is a great lesson for us all to never assume or judge another person.

Everyone has their own thoughts and opinions about putting medications into our children. It really needs to be a very personal matter. We need to listen to our doctors and consider their recommendation carefully since we cannot be allowed to put our child's health or life in danger by not taking necessary precautions. But I believe that sometimes doctors are a little too anxious to hand out prescriptions without trying safer alternatives first. You do not *have* to do something just because a doctor tells you to. Use some of your own judgment. Get a second or even third opinion. Research what is being suggested and decide if that is truly what is best for your child. I do not believe there is only one answer. I do feel that sometimes society is a little too anxious to "fix" something with medications when there may not be an actual problem in the first place. There are definitely times when medications need to be used and there are probably just as many times when other remedies may work just as well and be a lot safer. We need to be honest with our intentions and do our homework.

For some children there is a risk with *not* using medication, such as with diabetes and other serious chronic diseases that need medicinal management. There can often be vast difficulties and consequences for children if we cannot get things under control. Even children who may need medications for concentration or behavioral issues (such as ADHD) can suffer anything from poor school performance to low self-esteem and substance abuse without medication. When talking about the risks of using medication it should always be weighed against the risk of not taking it.

We chose to have our oldest son try a medication for his ADHD in seventh grade. We let it be his decision as well as ours, hoping it would make things better for everyone. His grades went almost immediately from D's and F's to A's and B's. But his personality went from happy, easy going and fun to melancholy, indifferent, or agitated. He had consistent headaches and no energy. We would definitely choose a happy, enjoyable son who felt good and was full of personality over one who gets A's and B's but is miserable. There is, fortunately, more than one way to get an education.

Different things work for different people and it is absolutely your choice to decide what works for your family. Some say that putting our kids on medication is just "taking the easy way out". I cannot imagine any parent has many easy decisions when it comes to helping their sick, disabled, or dysfunctional child cope in their everyday world. Any child with ASD or any other illness or disability has a tough life no matter what. With or without medications their life will always be harder than a typical person's.

I often feel that some people do not even believe me when I tell them Jesse has AS. Or if they do, they do not think it is that big of a deal. They are totally unaware of what a *big deal* it is for him. Jesse, along with every other person with AS, has to struggle every single day just to fit in and get through a day without any major anguish, confusion or distress. Many people with ASD are painfully aware of their shortcomings. They work overtime at school, home, jobs, and everywhere they go just to try and overcome their differences. Capitalizing on all the things your child does well is extremely beneficial to their self-esteem.

I was talking to someone a few years ago about my concerns of letting Jesse get a driver's license. This person, who knows Jesse (and that he has AS) and our family very well, actually sounded irritated with me when they responded, "You didn't make such a big deal out of R.J. driving, did you?" I was totally shocked that they just didn't even get it. I said, quite bluntly, "No, because R.J. does not have Asperger's!" It was as if they did not even consider for one minute why my concerns would be warranted. That was when I realized how little people actually know about AS, if anything. A friend of mine who has a son with AS wrote a little synopsis of what AS is for her family members, friends, son's teachers and anyone else who regularly interacts with her son. This let them know what it all means so they could warmly and thoughtfully include her son in their lives.

Others can be a great help when struggling with the challenges of raising a child with AS. We need each other. We just want to be cautious when handing out our personal advice or opinions.

CHAPTER TWELVE

Being a Parent

We have raised Jesse to know our love, self love, and God's love. We cannot possibly be with him to protect him at every moment, which he would not want anyway. We have to rely on his sense of self-worth and confidence to help him get through his life, just like all parents do. All parents have to realize that there will come a time when we really have to let go and have faith that our children will be able to make it on their own with what we have taught them and with the knowledge that they are loved and valued. Next comes the hardest question... *When* do we let go?

As a parent we have so many concerns. How do we deal with them all and let our child have his own existence separate from ours? One of a parent's biggest fears when their child has ASD is that he may regress. We feel like we cannot take our eyes off of them for one minute. We never want to see them go backward or lose a skill. For some reason mom's take it very personally when this happens. Maybe that is exactly why we have such a hard time letting them go in the first place. I find that I continuously make sure to give Jesse a lot of attention and I now know that it is partly to make sure that he continues to stay involved and connected. When he isn't talking much I try to get him to; if he is "lonely" in his room I get him to come and play a game with me; when he is outside playing basketball all by himself I will either go out and cheer him on when he gets baskets or I will actually try to play it with him, which is always a good laugh for him. I know he enjoys these interactions but I have to face the reality that I will not always be able to give them to him. When he is ready to leave our home to follow his own interests I obviously can't go with him, and I am not meant to either.

I know I baby Jesse more than I should. It is a mother's natural instinct to protect her child. Bob tries to tell me all the time that I need to give Jesse more space and I know my husband is absolutely right. I had a friend tell me once that one of the proudest moments for a parent should be when their child leaves the home, if the parent did their job right.

We must teach independence because it is the true root of lasting self esteem. Never do for your child what they can do for themselves. Any child. Give your child many opportunities to practice making decisions. Show him that you not only love him, but that you respect him, enjoy him and value him. Let him know that he is a person who deserves respect and the affection of others. Help him to build a foundation of self esteem and confidence from which he can one day venture into the world on his own. At a church event we went to recently Jesse made me feel really good because the boys had to say something about their mothers and he said, "She always makes sure I get everywhere I'm supposed to be and do what I need to do." It made me feel a little more significant, even though I know he really is capable on his own.

Naturally, all parents have things they worry about with their children. I guess some of the added things that parents with a child with AS face can be even more overwhelming. We think about "it" every single day. Who will treat them kindly and show them around? Who will help them know what they are expected to do and where they need to be? Will they ask for help if they need it? Will they call home if there is a substantial problem? Who will understand them?

People with speech and language problems or other cognitive deficits (as with AS) are so vulnerable. They often cannot tell you if something bad happens. They just do not know how to express themselves. Any parent knows how heart breaking and terrifying it is to not know what has happened to upset your child. Try to imagine having no way of getting them to tell you. People with AS are simply not wired the same and literally *cannot* tell us, even if they would like to. It is like the teen with AS who said if someone asks him an open question such as, "What do you want to eat?", there would be no way he could answer that. There are too many answers. We cannot just say to our AS child, "Tell me what is wrong" because there are too many answers. Most kids will come to their parents when they are extremely stressed or hurt looking for help and comfort. Jesse does not know how to get that and so he bears all his pain himself. When he moves away I won't ever know how he is *really* doing. Basically the only thing I can do is prepare him as much as possible for his approaching independence and take lots of comfort in knowing that I can always pray for his safety and happiness and know that he is still be being looked after. I need to have as much confidence in him as he has in himself.

As a parent we get a special gift, parental instincts. Don't let your pediatrician disregard your concerns if you feel something is not right about your child. If you feel something is wrong, it probably is. Too often parents are told "boys just talk later"; "older siblings are probably talking for him"; or other excuses for the delayed development. You know your child better than the pediatrician does. If your pediatrician will not take your concerns seriously than it is probably time to look for a new one. If your child does indeed have ASD, you need a doctor that will listen and sympathize with your concerns.

Genuinely all parents know how to show their child love and acceptance, but when you have a child with a disability you really have to put in overtime on building their self esteem. I believe everything happens for a reason and that Jesse was born into our home intentionally. We are not sure what he is thinking or feeling a lot of the time, but we do usually know what to say to him to comfort him and make him happy and secure. We just "get him". My friend Brandy, who also has a son with AS, says the same thing. I never was confused about how to treat him and how to raise him after learning of his AS. He is my son and I raise him like my other son and daughter…with just a few minor adjustments. Finding out he has AS explained a lot of things, but it did not change many. I think we always understood him and just accepted him for who he is. I do get frustrated when I am trying to get information from him and he does not respond or answer my questions. But I know to just let it go because he would if he could and he does when he can, which is good enough for me.

Sadly, there are many instances where children, teens, and even adults with ASD are abused because they do not know how to stop the abuse themselves or how to get help. Parents have to be vigilant in checking out teachers, caregivers and even new friends of their child's. Anyone associated with your child or teen should be someone you feel comfortable with, as much as possible. If your child or teen has friends, the likelihood that they are being picked on is greatly reduced.

Perhaps the hardest part of being the parent of a child with AS is to actually have the conviction and trust that your child really can often do what everyone else is doing. We cannot hold them back from their dreams and ambitions; we just can't.

Unless it is going to deeply harm them in some way, our kids need the freedom to take chances and succeed and accomplish their goals. They have to be able to live their lives. We all fail at some things and we all have difficulties at others, but we get right back up and move on. We all have disappointments as well as achievements. I will never be the one to tell Jesse he cannot do something.

There is an awful lot of guilt, uncertainty, and worry that often goes along with being a mom. Dad's love their child also and want what is best for them, but a lot of dads have to leave a lot of the decision making up to the mother simply because they often have other responsibilities to the family. It is often the dad who has to worry about expenses, which can keep him very busy. My husband is very supportive of me and would do anything for Jesse, but it is still my responsibility a lot of the time to know what needs to be done because my husband *is* very busy supporting our family so that I can be home with the children. He does not have time to research AS, so he leaves it up to me to get the facts and solutions. The mother is usually their child's full time researcher, biochemist, pharmacist, comrade, psychologist, educator, stylist, doctor, nutritionist, nurse, and chef. Moms are all these things anyway for their children, but it is multiplied dramatically with a disabled child. As a mother trust your instincts, you really do know more than you think you do. Keep an open-ended definition of what constitutes progress. Success for each child with AS is different. Do not compare your child, or yourself, to others. Every new skill and every new experience your child handles well is a great success. Two steps forward, one step back is still progress!

Depression for the parent can be triggered by very specific issues. You may feel that you are coping very well, are emotionally strong, and have come to terms with your child's disability. Then something as simple as an unkind comment or your child having a bad day at school is enough to bring back a flood of negative emotions and possibly feelings of hopelessness or depression. Do not feel that you have to carry your sadness in secret. It is critical to have your spouse, a good friend, a relative, or even a professional if needed, to support you.

I would give anything to be able to have a deep conversation with Jesse like I do my other two children. I believe that Jesse has the desire to communicate with us better also and to have someone understand what he is feeling, but he does not know how. I know that he feels so lonely sometimes and not being able to communicate like he would like to has to be part of the reason. Parents of a child with AS often have a feeling of one-sidedness in interactions with their child. Sometimes they feel as if they must carry the whole relationship to establish some meaningful connection. If the parent does not start the conversation or ask a specific question, their child may have very little to say or appear totally content on their own. Or, if the child is a "talker", it is often dedicated to their special interest. I know it takes Jesse a lot of effort to communicate with us when he needs to, unless he is just messing around. He can tease and be playful pretty easily. I can see that he wants to be a part of the group but he doesn't quite know how a lot of the time. It is as if he is nervous he will say the wrong thing, or maybe just nothing comes to mind. We all feel like that at times, but with people who have AS they are almost always self-conscious about appearing stupid, wrong, or at a total loss for words.

I remember one evening not too long ago when Jesse just came and plopped on the couch in the room Tonisha and I were in and he just sat in there with us while we were talking and just hanging out. I almost cried. He *never* used to do that! The only time he would stay in a room with any of us for more than a couple minutes was if there was a purpose, such as eating, watching television or something else concrete. That evening he just wanted to be with us. Ever since that day he has started to do it a lot more and it brings me so much joy. Parents of children with AS cannot take these bonding moments for granted because in some cases they do not happen very often.

We give Jesse as much attention as possible and I know sometimes it is still just not enough, but that is all we can do. We have two other children, a home, a marriage, our church, friends, extended family, Bob's job, and many other responsibilities. If you are honestly doing what you can to help your child with ASD then you simply cannot feel guilty, though we all still do. This is your life too and like the saying goes, "If mama's not happy, nobody's happy!" You have to have your own identity separate from your child's. You have to make sure you have interests and hobbies that are yours alone, and spend time on them...even if it isn't a lot. You and your spouse need to have time alone with each other, even if that only means 20 minutes each night before bed. Hopefully you can squeeze in more than that. Everyone wants and needs mom and it can be overwhelming sometimes. Just be sure not to neglect your own wants and needs all of the time. Sometimes the father's outlet is his job, but don't completely neglect other interests either. This life is meant for joy and we need to take every opportunity we can to have it.

Parents often find more help and support from talking to other parents of children with ASD than from professionals who often do not understand what they are going through. Other parents can give you ideas and helpful remedies that they have tried anywhere from medications, diets, therapies, to home life processes, rituals and schedules. Do remember that every child is different and talk to their doctor before trying a new medication or diet. It is amazing how many other parents you can meet in your same position just by talking and opening up to people. I was completely surprised at how many people know someone with AS when I started talking about it openly.

Parents of children or teens with AS have to be very observant of their child's health. These children are genuinely very oblivious of pain or sickness. They have very high physical thresholds and do not even notice most of the time when they are hurt. Jesse never complains of being sick and the couple of times we have heard him coughing incessantly did not even seem to concern him. I will force cough drops down him and he seems grateful, but he never asks for any on his own. He has probably only missed two or three days of school for sickness in his life, and that was only because *I* insisted he stay home. A fever could actually induce a seizure in a person with AS, so we are very lucky Jesse never gets fevers. As far as we know, he has only had one seizure in his life, which is very fortunate. As parents we need to keep an eye on their health and make sure they get check-ups once in a while since our child is not going to tell us if anything feels wrong.

One time Jesse came home from work with a pretty large cut on his arm that looked quite painful and he had no idea it was even there. Of course he doesn't ever know *how* they get there either. Many people with AS do not even notice excessive weather temperatures. Jesse will run out to our dog's kennel, through the snow, with bare feet all winter and not even be the least bit uncomfortable. Being the parents of a child with a disability adds a whole new load of responsibilities to keep them safe. But it is all worth it.

I read in the book: *A Different Kind of Perfect,* an insert from a mother with a son who has down syndrome that really touched me and explained exactly how I often feel about Jesse: An acquaintance of this mother was explaining to her fifth grade son how a child in his school had Down Syndrome and when the fifth grader asked who it was and his mom described him the boy said, "No mom, that boy is perfect. He is always happy and smiling and never angry."

Isn't perception everything? Everyone who knows Jesse would say that he is always happy and smiling also and never angry. Kids with any kind of disability have more right than anyone to be sad or angry, but they just aren't. They appreciate the little things. Anyone can have a typical child, but not everyone can have a "perfect" one.

CHAPTER THIRTEEN

Adulthood/Relationships

Throughout childhood and adolescence the person with AS typically builds a mental library of social experiences and social rules that help them immensely as they reach adulthood and obtain more independence. Each passing year Jesse is unquestionably becoming more and more outgoing and vocal. At a party we were at recently where he had a date with him I saw him making real efforts to have conversations with her. I also saw him give her quick glances when she would speak. I know it is still a great effort for him a lot of the time to know how to respond but his desire is to do what is expected. That is why he, and many other people with AS, go to great lengths to do what comes naturally to most of the rest of us.

As I said in the previous chapter, there are many people with AS who will talk your ear off. They can go on and on about a certain topic and not even realize that their audience is not thrilled with the knowledge they are sharing. It is very fortunate that by the time many have reached adulthood they have their mental library of experiences and rules to help them fit into the role of adulthood and be conventional. A thirty-two-year old rambling on and on at work about the solar system would not be much appreciated, unless they worked for N.A.S.A. of course.

Many people with AS are seen as shy, but there is a huge difference between being shy and feeling inadequate and most people with AS are not shy. When they do not speak up or they do not look you in the eye it really has nothing to do with being shy. Even as adults many people with AS are still very uncomfortable socially because they have so many obstacles in that area to overcome. Others are eventually able to socialize very well, with typical people unaware of the mental energy, support, understanding and education that is required for them to achieve such success.

Though many people with AS may appear to be shy, there are actually some who are not the least bit anxious around other people. They may just be uninterested or even unaware of how to interact with or approach others. And many of them just do not have any desire to. Some may not notice other people because they are too absorbed in other things, such as their own interests. People with AS take their special interests very seriously. On the other hand, many are very interested in getting to know others and to have friends. There is also a large percentage that want to have friends but feel inadequate and unsure of themselves and unsure of what they need to do. As a result, they actively avoid social contact. No matter what characteristics the person with AS shows, it is a mistake to assume that anyone with AS lacks affection. Some can be *very* affectionate toward those they know and care about. The lack of body language and communication may make them seem more distant than they actually are.

If children with AS hold onto their obsession as they reach adulthood, they can find success and joy in their jobs and livelihood. We can see in the AS person far more clearly than with any other child a predisposition for a particular profession from earliest youth. A particular line of work often grows naturally out of their special interests. A young child who has an obsession with computers could have a very successful career as a computer programmer or technician. Many kids with AS are gifted in music which could lead to composing, teaching, entertaining and other fields in that area. Mozart and Beethoven were both thought to have had AS. Many people with AS are very gifted writers and others have artistic abilities. There is a wide range of choices for most people with AS if they can channel their talents and knowledge into a career choice. In fact, there is no career that would be impossible for a person with AS. The list of professions held by people with AS includes teaching, politics, aviation, engineering, psychology, trades such as electricians and plumbers, mechanics, the arts, and wildlife. And this is by far not a comprehensive list. Our children with AS have a world of career opportunities open to them.

Some people with ASD stay away from jobs that are very social while others are in fields where their great knowledge is very beneficial shared openly, such as professors at universities or on the lecture circuit. Many people with AS are much more comfortable talking to a crowd than on a one on one basis because they do not have to worry about body language, innuendos, facial expressions or many other interface stumbling blocks. They also have a chance to prepare what they will say and if they have questions thrown at them it will likely be on the topic they are skilled in and can answer with confidence.

The job interview has to be one of the most difficult obstacles a person with AS ever has to endure. In the movie Adam, a story of a young man who has AS, Adam is very fortunate to find a wonderful lady to whom he becomes close with. She teaches him through role playing and modeling how to handle an interview. This assistance would be necessary and even critical for many people with AS if they are expected to have success at landing the job. Bob and I were recently fortunate enough to witness Jesse in a similar setting (although it was not for a job) where he was having all kinds of questions thrown at him. We were both very surprised and pleased at how well he did and how composed he seemed. We still want to prepare him as much as possible when an interview surfaces, but we are much more confident now after seeing how well he can handle himself and how respectful and prepared he appeared in that similar situation.

Dr. Temple Grandin (a well recognized scientist who also has ASD) says that 75 to 80 percent of people with ASD are in the workplace. Many of them remain undiagnosed or keep it quiet because it just does not matter. Chronic depression is associated with unemployment in typical people as well as people who have AS. Everyone needs a purpose.

People with AS can have relationships and fall in love. They just need to find the right person. Someone who understands them, is very patient, giving, and thoughtful; someone who loves him for who he is. This person would need to be a very noble person who is secure and confident in who they are themselves so that they can incorporate their desires to the success of the relationship. This is not to say that the neurotypical partner would not be receiving their share. A spouse with AS would most likely be very loyal, trustworthy, respectful, helpful, generous, kind, and devoted to them. The spouse without AS may need to find other resources or outlets to share deep feelings with when needed (a good friend or sibling). But on a day to day basis they would do just fine with shared feelings of compassion and the necessary dialogue with their AS partner.

Often some of the things that attract a lady to a man who has AS is his intellectual abilities and his degree of attention to her while first going out with him. The devotion can be flattering. His hobby or special interest can initially be perceived as endearing. Men with AS can also be admired for speaking their mind, having a sense of social justice and strong moral convictions. They are less motivated than other men to hang out with their male friends and therefore devote a lot of attention to the girl. Men with AS are often less concerned about their partner's body type than other men and also less concerned about age or cultural differences.

Having low self-esteem can greatly affect the choice of a partner for a woman with AS. They may set their expectations very low and as a result gravitate toward abusive men. I cannot stress the significance of good self-esteem in an adult with AS.

Some of the characteristics a man may find attractive in a woman with AS would include her social immaturity and naivety, her dependence on him. Many men have a natural paternal and compassionate quality where they thrive on being needed. We have to be careful here, though, as this could also be a harmful thing. Some instances of abuse may occur where there is too much dependency. There can also be the obvious physical attractiveness and admirable talents and abilities that will attract the man to her.

Men with AS may know that they need a partner who can act as an executive secretary to help with organizational problems and give them the continued emotional support that was supplied by their mother while living at home. They genuinely seek someone with strong moral values who will be dedicated to making the relationship work. Men with AS often seek a partner who can compensate for their difficulties in daily life while women with AS often want a partner with a personality similar to their own. They both generally feel more comfortable with someone who does not have a great need for a social life and does not seek frequent physical intimacy as well.

There are many potential problems in the marriage where one person has AS. As in every marriage, things often change after the honeymoon. During the dating stage the person with AS may have learned how to *do that part right* by observing others, television, books, etc. But when actual married life starts there is no way to be prepared for everything that will inevitably come up. The intentions are most likely good but sometimes that just doesn't matter. This is where a lot of patience, understanding, and counseling will help. Be fair and give the person a break, or many breaks. The person with AS will definitely have to give the non-AS partner plenty of breaks also. After all, no marriage is perfect and the problems that will be encountered with the AS partner are most likely not going to be as serious or hurtful as many of the traditional problems in a common marriage. It is a very safe bet that honesty and admiration for their spouse will always be the AS partners intentions.

Sometimes what may have been endearing while dating can later become a problem. Isn't that how it is for all of us? When I was dating my husband I thought it was so cute how he always teased his younger sisters. It is not so 'cute' now when he is always teasing *our* children! Another example would be when a girl is quite pleased to be getting all the attention she craves from her boyfriend because he does not care to be with other people. But it can become a problem when they are married for a while and she starts to desire more social inclusion and he still has no need or desire for that. She may not want to go to social gatherings without him and he may not want her to go at all. A compromise has to be made that they can both agree on such as possibly going more than he would like and less than she would. That is what we do in a marriage. The AS partner does need to realize and acknowledge that the non-AS spouse does require social interaction just for their general health and stability. It is important that the non-AS partner develop a network of friends to reduce the sense of isolation and enjoys the experience of social occasions with or without her AS partner when necessary. They cannot feel guilty when the partner is not there. It is likely that the partner with AS is totally content being left alone sometimes.

The person with AS needs to seek the kind of partner who understands them and can provide emotional support and guidance in the social world. Both partners would greatly benefit from relationship counseling from someone who has a wide knowledge of AS to make the unconventional relationship successful for both partners. There are also many good books now on the subject of marriage and AS.

In her book, *Asperger's in Love*, Maxine Aston describes a relationship with a partner having AS: "*In relationships AS men are often very honest, loyal and hardworking. Most will be faithful and remain with their chosen partner for life. They will give and offer love in the ways they can. If their partner understands AS they will appreciate that this giving will often take a practical form. It is unlikely that an AS man will be able to offer emotional support or empathic feelings. Some women will not be able to live with the emptiness and loneliness that this can bring.*"

People with AS clearly have problems understanding emotions within themselves and others and expressing emotions at an appropriate level for the situation. The person with AS may not express sufficient affection to meet the needs of his or her partner. A man with AS said, "We feel and show affection but often not enough or sometimes at the wrong intensity." The person with AS can be overly detached or overly attached. The typical partner would have to realize that during times of distress they may very well be left alone to 'get over it'. This is not because the AS partner does not care or is being insensitive, it is most likely because that is how they themselves would deal with a problem. In their minds the most effective emotional restorative is solitude.

People with AS have often described how a hug can even be extremely uncomfortable for them and does not make them feel better. Typical partners have described that hugging their AS spouse can be like 'hugging a piece of wood'. The person does not relax and enjoy such close proximity. For some people with AS they actually feel invaded and overwhelmed with intimacy. In some cases it is entirely the sensory experience that they cannot tolerate. The hug may be too light or too hard.

The non-Asperger's partner may also have difficulty having a romantic relationship with someone they often have to 'mother' and who may have the emotional maturity of an adolescent. In some relationships these things may not be a huge issue while in others it may cause vast problems. This is where counseling would be very much advised. There are many adults, most often women, who are very content with a virtually platonic marriage. That is helpful since it is less than one fourth of women with the AS. It would presumably be much harder for a non-Asperger's man to live that way. Sadly, though, even women who do not necessarily need total interaction still need and desire closeness in other physical ways such as kissing and holding each other. The couple will have to find what works for them to satisfy each other.

The non-AS partner deserves admiration for their ability to commit themselves to the relationship when three main factors may not be present: deep communication, empathy, and often a lack of physical closeness. (Not all people with AS reject physical intimacy.) Among their many attributes was belief in their partner, remaining faithful to the relationship, understanding that he or she 'can't' rather than 'won't', and an ability to imagine and have compassion for what it must be like to have Asperger's.

There are three requisites for a successful relationship where one of the partners has AS. The first is that both partners acknowledge the diagnosis and know as much about it as possible. The person with AS can have a realization of how their actions, attitudes and behaviors affect their partner and try to cope with needed changes and mutual understanding. It should not always be the non-AS partner sacrificing. There are many things the AS person can learn and adjust to. That leads to the second requisite. After learning as much as possible, both partners need to have the drive and desire to change in an effort to make things run more smoothly for both. The third requisite is access to relationship counseling modified to accommodate the profile of abilities of the partner with AS.

A lot of parents of children with ASD worry that their child will never get married or have children. These exceptional people have so much to offer to a marriage and a family! They are thoroughly devoted, trustworthy, reliable, honest and giving individuals. They also usually have a very good sense of humor, which we can all use in a marriage. Jesse is 100% committed when he is involved in something. He goes to work every day, on time, and gives it his all. He does everything his religion asks of him. He has always been an excellent student. He knows right from wrong and does everything he can to be a good person. I feel that if our children with AS are able to learn the basics of living independently and they have a support system of friends and family, nothing should stop them from having everything typical adults have, including their own family to share their life with!

New concerns will most likely come up when children come into the family. The non-AS parent may feel as though they are a single parent at times. I have no doubt that the AS partner will be just as capable as the spouse to take care of physical needs of the children, but emotional needs may be a bigger challenge. They want to; they just may not have the capabilities. The person with AS *does* feel kindness and concern, they just do not always know how to express it or what is expected of them. They also have a very hard time putting feelings and thoughts into dialogue. This is one aspect of family life that truly will be more on the non-AS partner's shoulders, and as I have said many times, it is imperative that they have people they can confide in and go to for help and interaction. In the perfect world we would all be very content and fulfilled solving all of our problems together as couples, and maybe that is the way it should be. But in all reality, most typical people even talk to a friend or parent about children or spouse issues when they need some new perspective and understanding.

The entire family may have some different things they need to tolerate and learn to live with that go alone with having a member with AS. There may be certain smells or noises that are just not tolerable. There could be times when a social function may be ended abruptly when the AS parent has had as much as they can handle. Meticulous routines may need to be followed. The child may sometimes need to play the role of the adult to guide the AS parent along in some situations. In Liane Holliday Willey's book: *Pretending to Be Normal,* she tells of how her children let her know what is appropriate in public and what is not, and she is totally good with that. And, they are also good with letting her be herself, when it's not *too* embarrassing such as her screaming out at a sporting event with her hands over her ears, "How do you people handle all this noise?" Children who are fortunate enough to have one parent, or both, with

AS will always be loved, cared for, and secure. It just might be shown in less conventional ways. A positive attitude and alternative way of handling life is imperative.

CHAPTER FOURTEEN

New Recognition for AS

The general public seems to have this unrealistic impression that basically everyone with AS is young and this is a relatively new disease, or there aren't nearly as many adults with it as children. Not true. Although AS was not much heard of until the early 1990's, it has been around for a very long time, possibly even centuries. We do seem to focus more on children, but in reality there is currently becoming a surge of referrals of adults for a diagnostic assessment for AS. The reason is simply that there is so much more information and recognition of it now than as little as five years ago. There are even many television shows and movies that have characters in them playing a person who has AS or Autism.

People who have AS themselves and those who see signs in a loved one are learning what those things could mean because they are learning information that has not been previously given. Many couples are starting to question if their spouse may have AS because that would explain his or her difficulties with empathy and social skills, among other things. While it is possible that some may have it, we have to be realistic and realize that there are so many different possibilities. We cannot start labeling everyone who does not cry at funerals with AS. Many males have a natural characteristic of 'not listening' or not showing their feelings as much as females do. We can't jump straight to AS on that alone. But now that we do have much more information and can learn what the real indicator's and concern's are, many more people who have always felt like they belong on another planet can finally have some real answers.

Most people know very little about AS, if anything at all. Parents of children with AS generally know more about the disorder than even their doctors do. In fact, many doctors know very little about it at all. I was both disappointed and pleased with Jesse's most recent doctor. This particular doctor admitted to me that when he saw that Jesse's paperwork said that he had AS he didn't know much about it. That is what disappointed me. I was also quite stunned that this same doctor gave the impression that he thought it was a relatively new disease and not very common. What kind of world do we live in where even our medical field knows very little about AS when it is affecting one in 100 children in the 21st century? AS has actually been around for at least a century(though there was not an actual name for it until the 1940's). AS is a lot more prevalent than childhood diabetes and doctors know plenty about that disease. I was very pleased, though, when the doctor next told me that he went home that same evening after our first visit and studied everything he could find about it and truly wanted to know more. I would certainly hope that AS has become part of the curriculum in medical school by this point.

As well as medical doctors, *every* teacher from pre-school through college should be educated on what AS is and the different attributes associated with it. It is imperative that teachers understand the different ways these students learn along with many other issues from social to cognitive skills. Teachers need to have a basic knowledge of the student's delayed theory-of-mind abilities. Some children with AS need to be in special classes, but there are many who will do very well in standard school settings if the teacher has the knowledge they need and shows an empathetic understanding of the child. Many children with AS, Jesse included, can do quite well on their own throughout the school years without any special help. But many others will fail miserably if the teacher does not recognize certain issues associated with their AS.

All of society needs at least a simple basic understanding of AS and other ASD's since it has a tremendous impact on the child's ability to journey towards a productive, independent adulthood. A general public knowledge would also greatly benefit adults with it in ways of employment opportunities and more compassion. We can appreciate unique contributions to our society and experience joy and hope by learning so much from someone as amazing as Jesse. He sees the world in such a more simple and good way than many of us do. He is a very positive person and is determined to have a happy and fulfilling life.

How many wonderfully quirky and surreal stories are hidden beneath some of these individuals' idiosyncrasies? Wouldn't it be fascinating to have more biographies and personal stories shared from these kids, and adults, about what they go through in their lives and the ways they view the world? Fictional stories coming from the mind of someone with AS would also be fascinating. Generally, people with AS are exceptionally intelligent but they have communication problems which makes it harder to share their thoughts and intellect vocally. It would be wonderful if we could get them to write things down more and expose their thoughts, feelings, and ideas that way. I believe that many very successful writers may have ASD, which could in fact contribute to what makes them such compelling and enjoyable authors.

Sadly, many ASD's are surrounded by myths and generalizations that are rarely appropriate. The common belief that people with an ASD, particularly autism, never express emotion, never smile or laugh, never make eye contact, never display affection and never talk are truly myths. Children with ASD who develop selective mutism in their early years can talk fluently when relaxed, such as at home; but when in public their level of anxiety may be so severe that they are unable (not unwilling) to speak.

Family members and friends were shocked to learn that Jesse used to talk up a storm at home when he was younger to the point that we would actually have to tell him to quiet down. Most of them rarely heard him talk at all. Even now as a young adult I will hear him talk a lot with his friends in a comfortable setting but be pretty much silent in a larger gathering. There are also many people with ASD who are very comfortable speaking in public. Just as every other individual is different with their own unique gifts and personalities the same is true for those with ASD. Every person with ASD manifests the disorder in his or her own unique way.

Unfortunately, many people consider people who have AS "oblivious" or "absentminded" and assume that they simply do not notice the behavior of others. As most parents can attest, that is hardly true. The pain and humiliation children with AS feel is acute and very real. Every day is a challenge for them, and very exhausting. I can only imagine how confusing some people and situations are to those who have AS. Someone with AS generally does not understand any reason to ever hurt anyone or lie or break laws. Most people with AS are very caring and good citizens. There is also the misconception that people with AS do not have much empathy, but that is not true either. They have very deep feelings, they just do not know what they should be feeling in some situations and other times they do not know how to express what they are feeling.

There are many adults with ASD who look and seem normal in many ways, but who still have difficulty dealing with some of the basic aspects of everyday life. Many people believe that AS and Autism are the same thing...They aren't. Fortunately this is all starting to change. It always amazes me that it took until Jesse was almost fourteen years old for anyone to mention there was something different about him. I remember one instance when he was spending the night at his cousin's house and my sister told me later that she was getting quite frustrated because she kept asking him what he wanted on his hamburger and he would just smile and not answer her. That was the first time she had ever seen anything strange enough in his behavior to mention it to me (and he was thirteen!). But I never noticed anything either.

Research has come a long way with ASD's over the past few years. Although it is very likely that they have existed for hundreds of years, until recently no one had thought to create a distinct category or name for it because our culture (social, medical, and educational) was not ready for it. Asperger's is not even in the 1999 edition of Webster's Dictionary. This is the best time to have an ASD because these individuals are finally getting the recognition, compassion and acceptance they deserve. There is so much more help available now than even a decade ago. However, what is still extremely frustrating and unwarranted is that the programs that *are* available to help these kids are only for the very rich or the very poor. You have to be in the poverty level to qualify for help or you have to be very wealthy to pay for them on your own. Where does that leave the majority who are in between? The health and well being of any child should not have to be a financial decision.

The government needs to realize that it would be a much smaller cost to help these children become adjusted in childhood to where they can develop some amount of independence than have to support them all throughout their adulthood. The good news is that the more recognition and research ASD receives, it will likely open more doors and opportunities in the near future which will also likely include a wider range of promising financial help. Along with more research, programs and help, there will be many more choice outcomes including independent living, further education, satisfying careers and even marriage and children for these individuals if that is what they desire. My main objective is just for AS to become more recognized, understood and appreciated which I also believe will happen as society learns more about it.

There are many creative and very talented people with AS. Without them, the world would be much less interesting. Albert Einstein's teacher once told him that if they opened up his head they would not find a brain, just a lump of fat! We all know how intelligent he really was. He was recognized to have AS.

Virtually everyone with High-Functioning Autism or AS improves with time and age. They generally become more interested in social contact, and they gain new or increasing conversation skills. In all studies conducted this far, good verbal ability and average or above average intelligence in childhood seemed to be the key to predicting a good outcome in adulthood. There are so many reasons to have hope.

Many believe that autism has become an epidemic since the 1990's. What may be called an epidemic could really be just a reflection of a change in the way a culture perceives a condition or disease. We can only hope that something good will actually come from labeling autism an epidemic. It is human nature to stand up and take notice when that word gets tossed into the headlines.

I do not know if ASD's are any more prevalent than they were 50 or 100 years ago or if they are just gaining more recognition and understanding from the general population along with science. But as I point out in the chapter "*Causes*", if it truly is an epidemic then that very thing would prove that it is not exclusively a genetic disease. That would give us much hope because if we could find the environmental factors responsible and remove them we would very possibly eliminate ASD someday.

Today we are able to see a news story on the topic of ASD's nearly every month when just a couple of years prior we hardly ever heard anything about them. All the attention and recognition it gets can only lead to good. More understanding, more curiosity, more research, more monetary backing, more compassion, more support.

I can say that I would have been very well served to have known about ASD just fifteen years ago when Jesse was young and also when I was running a daycare. It would have benefited more than one of the children under my care I am sure. Now that I am able to recognize AS, I am convinced that I had a couple of children in my day care that had it. I remember one boy in particular who I'll call Sam. I, regrettably, always thought he was just being extremely difficult and assumed that he was very spoiled at home. Sam, at the tender age of five would tell me *exactly* how his lunch was to be prepared. He insisted on bringing his own brand of hot dogs from home each day (which was the *only* thing he would eat) and he would instruct me on how long…to the second…they should be cooked in the microwave. If I went even a second over he would get very upset and refuse to eat them. He was very sharp for a five year old and there was no fooling him. Truthfully, the only reason I even catered to his egocentric behavior was because it was much easier, and quicker, than trying to force feed him anything else and going through a scene every day while the other children had to wait. He also would have a major melt down and act as if he were in pain if anyone touched him at all. I did think Sam was a little unusual, but how would I have ever recognized AS in him when I didn't even know my own son had it? The two of them were completely different from each other. I had never even heard the word Asperger's before. I had another little boy in my daycare who was three and refused to talk. He would just point at things. But other than that he seemed absolutely 'normal'. His mother was even concerned but it never crossed either of our minds that he may have ASD.

In the past, and still even the present, in some countries, anyone different was automatically considered crazy. Families would either put the person in an institution or they would hide them in their homes and not let anyone know the individual even existed. We are very fortunate to live in a more progressive day and age.

It would bring relief to so many parents and families to find answers for their loved ones quirkiness, misunderstandings, social ineptness and other issues if more people just knew there is such a thing as AS and what it includes. The ASD scale is very complex and covers a very wide range. You cannot compare your child to anyone else because even children or adults with AS are just as unique and complex as anyone else. We, of course, do not want to start labeling everyone who has any unique signs of individuality, but we do need to acknowledge that there are many people who would be much happier and better accommodated if they had some answers to their questions. There is a huge difference between a two year old who occasionally throws tantrums and a two year old who is virtually *always* in a state of anxiety. When your child is eight years old and still does not understand how to use the telephone it could be a reason to question. If your child has many digestion and bathroom issues along with clear signs of detachment or numerous other social issues, maybe it is time to consider ASD. Of course, not everyone who has intestinal problems or appears shy has ASD. You just have to be honest with yourself and acknowledge when there is clearly something going on.

I am sure by the time you have reached this far in the book you will most likely have some idea whether your loved one has an ASD of some type, if you did not already know. The signs are so clear when you know what you are looking for. For example, when Jesse was two years old and the Skittles commercial came on the television… he was toddling around the room seemingly not even paying any attention to the television when just out of the blue he softly said, to no one, "Taste the rainbow." We all laughed and thought it was so cute. It was not until many years later that I would recognize that that was echolalia. If I had known about ASD back then I might have paid more attention and questioned that. Many children and even adults with AS copy things they hear, which is called echolalia. Many times we as their parents will not even realize that is what they are doing. Sometimes it is much more obvious such as when they continuously repeat a scene from a favorite movie, book or cartoon, etc.

After watching Jesse through the years and doing all my research for this book I have learned three encouraging and noble things about these individuals…

1. They truly do the best that they can.
2. They instinctively treat their own disorder.
3. They are very loveable and enjoyable people.

CHAPTER FIFTEEN

Accepting and Welcoming Aspergers

I can only convey what I have learned and experienced personally from raising a son with AS along with all of the books and information I have read and studied, and what I have learned from talking with other parents who have a child with it. The people that can help us understand it best are those who actually have it, by describing their thoughts and feelings. Sadly that is often one of the hardest things for them to do. I was able to find a few short statements that help us appreciate a little bit of what it means to have AS. This chapter starts off with quotes from teenagers who have it and want people to know what they go through every day of their lives. I feel this will be a big eye opener to most of us and help us to know how to help them better. I hope you enjoy reading from "their eyes".

"You might feel like a bad friend or flaky because you never call friends to do anything. Other people might not see you that way but that's how you feel anyway. You just can't help being drained by most kinds of social interaction."

"It's hard for people to understand why I ask something that boils down to 'common sense.'"

"We have to always fake normal to live in the cutthroat world that is politics. It's very exhausting."

"If I am around others and I am feeling sad or I need to look empathetic, I mentally have to think about how to display that emotion on my face. That emotion does not appear automatically."

"Just because you can't see how I feel doesn't mean that I don't feel."

"It truly wears you down to use diplomatic skills all day. I come home exhausted mentally, not so much physically, every single day from work. I'm happy my cat seems to know how I feel—no need to fake there!"

"I hate having such a hard time being able to start a regular conversation. Asking someone how their dog is or how their daughters dance recital was is so difficult. Once passed 'how are you' I am at a complete loss as to how to carry on a conversation."

"I hate it when just one little thing messed up on my routine throws me off for the entire day! I then can't remember what I'm supposed to be doing and have to pretty much give up and wait for the next day!"

"You go through your whole life knowing something is off about you but don't have the skills to communicate how it's affecting you."

"You spend most of your time trying to learn the "rules" to a world that doesn't seem to care about them anyway."

"I don't even know when a girl is flirting with me or when someone is making fun of me."

"I can hear what others say and know what the words mean but I don't pick up on the 'non-verbal' part so I don't always understand what they are saying."

"Some things people could do to help me are explain things when I don't understand, not bullying or setting me up, stand up for me if others are being unkind."

"All kids want friends and I'm no different. Try to be patient and kind. After all, it could easily have been you who was born with a problem. None of us can choose our genes, our parents or where we are born."

"I always feel lost and alone."

"People with AS can like and love people, like everyone else. We may not show our feelings much on the outside, but that doesn't mean that we don't have them."

"My cousin died a few days ago and I don't know how to act at her funeral. I know people will be crying and I can't cry. I don't want to be seen as unfeeling."

"One of the major problems I have with my AS is the in-ability to allow people to touch me. I've been in three relationships and they all ended quickly as soon as touching became involved. And I'm only talking about simple hugs and holding hands."

"Having Asperger's does not make me less human or less emotional."

"When I am asked what I would like to eat or drink by another person it is impossible for me to answer. The question is too big. I have to know what is available to make a choice."

"Often when someone with Asperger's recognizes that you are upset they won't do anything even though they want to. It's because they don't know what to do and they don't want to do the wrong thing."

Descriptions of love from the eyes of Asperger's:

An attempt to connect to the other person's feelings.
Companionship.
Someone to depend on to lead you in the right direction.
Tolerant, loyal, allows space.

There is always a logical explanation for the apparently eccentric behavior of people with AS. Everything they say or do comes from reasoning and truth. Their way of thinking makes more sense and is much more honest than most of ours is. How many wives with AS would ask their husband if they look fat in something when they already know if they do or don't? How many husbands with AS would tell their wife they will be home right after the game and then get there two hours later? None. When an excited child with AS flaps his hands joyfully it makes a lot more sense than someone who is overwhelmed with happiness keeping a straight face and staying silent as we often do...at least until we're out of public view.

People with AS are very honest, literal, philosophical, insightful individuals. They say what they mean and they mean what they say. Sometimes, such as in Jesse's case, they just don't say a whole lot. A lot of the time they see no reason to make small talk and they have no idea why anyone else would either. That makes sense. It is just niceties and awkward silence fillers. Wouldn't it be nice if we could all relax in silence and not feel like we have to fill every gap with unnecessary chatter? Shouldn't a friendly smile be just as appreciated as "How are you?" It is comparable to when you are first dating and you feel awkward if there is prolonged silence...more than three seconds. But by the time you have been married for two years you can eat an entire dinner, at a restaurant no less, without peeping one sound or even looking at each other. People with AS can do that right from the beginning!

Where would we be without the astounding contributions from the many brilliant and gifted people said to have had AS? Albert Einstein, a pure genius including his mathematical equations regarding light and energy; Isaac Newton, one of the foremost intellects of all time including his development of the theory of color, his genius in mathematics and astronomy, and his unearthing of gravity; Benjamin Franklin, one of the founding fathers of the United States of America. He was a scientist, an inventor and most widely recognized for his discovery of electricity. Leonardo Da Vinci gave us the Mona Lisa and The Last Supper along with many other brilliant works of art. And, unknown to most, his geological and paleontological observations foreshadow many later breakthroughs. There are many other infamous people said to have had AS that contributed so much to our world, and there are many still alive and contributing today. Significant advances in science and the arts have been attributed to individuals who have a different way of thinking and who possess many of the cognitive characteristics associated with AS. Some children with AS, especially girls, can develop the ability to use imaginary friends or characters and worlds to write quite remarkable fiction. Hans Asperger is quoted as saying, "Not everything that steps out of line, and thus 'abnormal', must necessarily be inferior." Many people with AS would not want to be cured because that would be like erasing them and replacing them with a different person. People with AS are genuinely happy with who they are. We all need to accept ourselves that way.

Many typical children and teens who are naturally understanding, kind, and "maternal" may find children with AS pleasant and enjoyable and can be tolerant of their quirks, which means their friendships can last for many years. Jesse still has a lot of the same friends he made when we first moved to our current home nine years ago, and the new ones he has made also stick around. There are a lot of very caring and accepting adolescents who realize that he has so much to offer to the friendship that an occasional awkward moment means nothing. He is really fun to be around and very kind and loyal to his friends. So what if he is not one to hold a long conversation, he says what he needs to most of the time.

Most people do not advertise their AS, so it is unknown how wide spread it is. But we do know that a lot of people with AS have exceedingly exceptional gifts and talents which contribute immensely to our society. In modern society we need and benefit greatly from the talents of people with AS. We should acknowledge and celebrate the values that these individuals share.

AS impacts every aspect of the person's life. It is a gift that brings with it many incredible traits. It also brings some unusual difficulties for these individuals as well. We can all show more understanding and compassion to people with AS, or anyone else with a feature that makes them "different". Just like one of the teens said, "It could easily have been you or I born with a problem."

While growing up I always had a dream of becoming an author of teen fiction; but as I got married and had my children that dream faded as I pursued other avenues. I would have never imagined I would someday be writing this kind of a book. But now I believe it is my responsibility, and my honor, to do what I can to help educate society about ASD's, particularly AS. I want to do this for Jesse and every other child, teen, or adult who just wants to be understood better. I never cared to make any money from this or even be well known...I just want my book to reach as many hands as possible so I can let more people know all about these amazing people who have a very mysterious gift called Asperger's.

Before having Jesse, raising him, reading everything I could get my hands on about ASD, and talking to others living with it, I did not know anything about AS. I had never even heard the word. It is way past time for society to know more about this complex disorder that affects more than 1 in every 100 children! I believe there are many out there, including adults, who have it and do not even realize they do. Maybe something I said in this book will help someone understand themselves or someone they love better and realize what might be the reason for some of their unconventional behaviors. Maybe someday, with the help of everyone who knows and loves someone with ASD, the world will be much more educated, more qualified, and more able to offer helpful advice, opinions, and support. Maybe society will be able to accept and even appreciate each others' differences and acknowledge the valuable assets we each offer to one another. Maybe someday there will not even be a need for the label Asperger's! We can always hope.

RECOMMENDED READING:

The Complete Guide to Asperger's Syndrome; Tony Atwood; Jessica Kingsley Publishing

Ten Things Every Child with Autism Wishes You Knew; Ellen Notbohm

Louder Than Words; Jenny McCarthy

Mother Warriors; Jenny McCarthy

Son Rise: Barry Kaufman

The Oasis Guide To Asperger's Syndrome; Patricia Romanowski Bashe, M.S. Ed., Barbara L. Kirby; Crown Publishers New York

Parenting Your Asperger's Child; Alan Sohn, Ed.D and Cathy Grayson, M.A.

Unstrange Minds, Remapping the World of Autism; Roy Richard Grinker; www.basic books.com

A Parent's Guide to Asperger's Syndrome and High Functioning Autism; Sally Ozonoff, P.H.D., Geraldine Dawson, P.H.D. and James McPartland; The Guilford Press.

Kids in the Syndrome Mix of ADHD, LD, Asperger's, Tourette's, Bipolar, and more!; Martin L. Kutscher M.D.; Jessica Kingsley Publishers.

A Child's Journey out of Autism; Leeann Whiffen; Sourcebook, Inc.

Changing the Course of Autism; Bryan Jepson M.D., with Jane Johnson; Sentient Publications.

A Different Kind of Perfect; Cindy Dowling, Neil Nicoll, Bernadette Thomas; Shambhala Publications, Inc.

Pretending to be Normal, Living with Asperger's Syndrome; Liane Holliday Willey